"GET ME THE WHITE HOUSE!"

*The untold story of Victor Frenkil's rise from
immigrant obscurity to prominence in
the turbulent worlds of business and politics*

By Jacques Kelly
and Anthony Weir

GATEWAY PRESS, INC.
Baltimore, MD   2006

Please direct all correspondence and book orders to:
Victor Frenkil, Jr.
1030 E. Patapsco Ave.
Baltimore, MD 21225

Library of Congress Control Number 2006905807
ISBN 0-9776907-0-9

Published for the author by
Gateway Press, Inc.
3600 Clipper Mill Rd., Suite 260
Baltimore, MD 21211-1953

www.gatewaypress.com

Printed in the United States of America

*For all those who helped
Victor Frenkil achieve what he did —
including his wife, family, friends,
and especially his employees. And to
his son, Bruz, who loved enough to
turn his father's dream into a reality.*

Contents

Victor Frenkil of Baltimore Contractors in one of his favorite photos of himself, captured here using the business weapon he most favored and most frequently used in his relentless drive for victory — the telephone.

Foreword

"Man can will nothing unless he has first understood that he must count on no one but himself; that he is alone...with no other destiny than the one he forges for himself on this earth."

Jean Paul Sartre

I met Victor Frenkil in 1949 when my older brother Kit and I, at the ages of 15 and 13, were invited to spend two weeks with his sons, Bruz (Victor Jr.) and Len, at the Frenkil summer cottage on the steep banks of the Magothy River in Cape St. Claire, Maryland, just opposite Gibson Island.

I don't remember much of Victor from that visit, probably because — busy as always — he was rarely there. But his son, Bruz, and I developed a friendship that would last a lifetime (indeed 56 years as of this writing). As a result, I was invited back often and, at the age of 15, spent the summer working for Victor at Baltimore Contractors (BCI) and bunking with Bruz at the Frenkil's gracious estate, Wilton, in Owings Mills. That summer, Bruz worked a BCI construction site pushing Georgia buggies filled with cement while I worked for Mary Lambrow in the filing department (Mary was sister to Victor's right-hand administrative assistant and éminence grise, Virginia Lambrow).

Victor was not an easy person to warm to, at least from a

teenager's point of view. He was all business, generally coming home well after the family had finished dinner, spending most of his time while home on the telephone, enraptured by interests that had nothing to do with us budding hormone-heavy teenagers. He did not display much interest in children — at least that I could see.

As I came to learn, Victor was an unusual human being, a great character. In fact, I wrote a paper about him for my sophomore English Class at preparatory school. The theme, assigned by the professor, was "the most unforgettable character I've met". Vic (as I called him) qualified easily.

I wrote the paper about something that happened while I was visiting and working at his company, a trip to the office one morning when Vic's chauffeur didn't show up on time. So Vic decided to drive, something he almost never did. We climbed into his long black Chrysler limousine and set off. I was terrified, since he seemed to pay no attention to his driving (every teenage boy has driving on the mind, and I could not fail to be critical).

He turned the radio on to listen to the morning news. He had a mug of coffee or juice in one hand, which he would sip noisily. Then he spread the morning paper out over the steering wheel, two pages wide, and began to read the latest news. And, given his penchant for music, he began to sing — all the while racing down Reisterstown Road toward the office. The fact that we arrived safely still seems a miracle to me.

I spent many happy times with Vic and his family at Wilton and at the Magothy River cottage. During my second visit, I fell in love with Janet, his eldest child, who was about five years my senior (a lifetime when you're 14) and stunningly beautiful (not surprisingly, the love was unrequited). I also developed a close relationship with Margaret, Bruz' mother, who was one of the kindest, gentlest, most giving people I had ever met. I remember describing her as "having no sharp edges whatsoever", one of the reasons she was such a perfect match for Vic. I became, by mutual acceptance, her "fifth child".

Vic once asked my father to write and produce his first company brochure, which my father was happy to do (for free) after all the hospitality I had enjoyed. Vic proved to be a constant meddler, challenging everything my father did, asking for rewrites, micro-managing as always. My father, not happy having his professional talents questioned constantly by someone thoroughly unskilled in the art of communication, wisely realized there was only one solution: He sent Vic a bill for $1,000 for work-in-progress. Vic never touched the brochure again, mentioning proudly to some of his colleagues that "Our brochure is being done by Walter Weir, one of America's greatest ad men, and it's costing me $1,000". Suddenly the work had value — and Vic respected that, so he left it alone.

I saw Vic over the years as a consequence of my friendship with Bruz. He was always curious as to what I was doing professionally (I was then a creative director at Ogilvy & Mather, an advertising agency based in New York) and always asked me how much money I was being paid, probably assessing me as he tended to do with everyone he met and viewing compensation as a measure of whatever talent I had.

Vic began to invite me to occasional business reviews he held at Baltimore Contractors, always after hours, at which the managers of the various businesses he owned would report their progress in tedious detail. This was done, I believe, to interest me in his world because, shortly thereafter, he began to suggest that Bruz and I would make a first-rate team were we to work together, hinting that, ultimately, we would take over Baltimore Contractors as he began to pull out (which, of course, he never really did). This suggestion was made on many occasions but was never accompanied by a specific offer. It is just as well that he didn't make an offer, because I would never have considered subjecting my professional career to such a domineering micro-manager — in spite of my respect for him and my considerable affection for his son. (His daughter, Janet, recently told me that Vic tried to hire many of the people he met. He apparently believed that success was achieved by extended families working together, all under his roof — with, of course, emphasis on the "his".)

Meanwhile Bruz, working at Baltimore Contractors but desperate to get out from under his father's heavy thumb, left BCI and moved to a subsidiary company which he eventually bought and turned into Jarvis Steel & Lumber, a business at which he prospered (and, more important, enjoyed).

Every once in a while, Vic would call me in New York for advice, usually when he was in trouble and concerned about what was being said about him in the newspapers. I remember telling him what I had once advised a Maryland politician for whom I had done some consulting: "In public life, there is no such thing as truth. There is only what people perceive to be true". Given that he was under attack for questionable dealings over a government job, and literally was fighting city hall, I urged him not to stir the pot. He followed the advice and kept his head down (even though I did not send him a bill).

Many years later, I learned from Bruz that his dad wanted a biography written as his legacy. Typically, Vic had hired a writer or two on the cheap and had received precisely what he paid for, which was very little. Several drafts were written, but the book never got beyond the preliminary stages. The project languished.

Shortly after Vic's death, Bruz called me to ask for help with the book. It was very much like Bruz: He simply had to honor his father's request (none of Bruz' siblings seemed interested in the project). I told him I was far too busy to do it, that we would need to hire someone who was a professional writer and, with any luck, knew something about Baltimore and the Maryland political scene. I made it clear that I was more than willing to act as editor, to rewrite what I thought needed improvement, to add where necessary, but that vast amounts of time were required to assemble the story, to dig through old newspapers, to track down and interview many who knew Vic, to pour over boxes of old records — a daunting task.

The search began. We interviewed several writers and rejected them. Then we had the good fortune to come across Jacques Kelly, whom I invited to Philadelphia so that he and I could meet to discuss the task. Both Bruz and I thought he could do the job. He was, to begin with, a professional writer, a journalist who understood the concept of reporting. Given his position at *The Baltimore Sun*, he had access to reams of files that no one else could have sourced. And, as a journalist who had worked the Baltimore scene for many years, he was aware of many of the characters who would be featured in the biography. Further, by sheer serendipity, he was a Baltimore history buff.

We hired him, and the result of an enjoyable, three-way collaboration among Jacques, Bruz and me is now in your hands.

The fact that the book exists at all is a tribute to the determination of Bruz, whose remarkable sense of duty would not permit him to do otherwise. Bruz has driven the project. Bruz has funded the project. Bruz has finished the project. Now that the book is printed, Vic must be smiling, having known from the beginning that Bruz would not let him down.

Working on *"Get Me The White House"* led me to understand and appreciate Vic far more than I had previously. I found his unfolding story fascinating, his character unique, his accomplishments remarkable. He was a driven man.

As someone also driven, I have been intrigued by what it is that motivates people and makes them try harder than their peers. I was never quite sure what it was that drove Vic, and would guess that it was a combination of factors. First was the fact that he was a Jew in a world that was essentially anti-Semitic. Second was that he was shorter than many of his peers, probably about five feet, eight inches. Third was his tendency to be a loner, unwilling (and probably afraid) to open up emotionally in front of others, a kind of self-imposed isolation that went beyond shyness.

Whatever, he capitalized on these motives to outwork, outcompete and outperform most of his peers, constantly proving himself to others (and, more important, to himself).

I came to understand Victor Frenkil as a fellow human being with whom I had traits in common, as opposed to the distant father of a friend. In the end, I knew him in much greater detail, and I liked what I saw.

I was privileged to have known him and the fascinating world in which he flourished, and hope you will arrive at a similar conclusion by the time you finish the book. If so, his lifelong wish will have been achieved — and that matters almost as much to me as it does to Bruz.

Anthony Weir

weirmarketing@comcast.net

July 2005

I. The Melting Pot

*"America is God's Crucible, the great
Melting-Pot where all the races of Europe
are melting and re-forming!"*
　　　　　　　　　Israel Zangwill

On Monday, 14 September, 1908, there appeared in *The
Baltimore Sun* (which sold on the newsstands for one
penny) the following quotation:

> *"The true friend of reform, the true foe of abuses,
> is the man who steadily perseveres in righting wrongs,
> in warring against abuses, but whose character and
> training are such that he never promises what he can-
> not perform, that he always a little more than makes
> good what he does promise, and that, while steadily
> advancing, he never permits himself to be led into
> foolish excesses which would damage the very cause
> he champions."*

Those words could have been spoken prophetically about a
person who, on that very same day, came into the world:
Victor Frenkil. (As it turns out, they were spoken by President
Theodore Roosevelt about Judge William Howard Taft, whom
Roosevelt had endorsed to succeed him in the White House.
In fact, they were to be more descriptive of Victor Frenkil than

they were to be of Taft.)

Victor was born into a busy family. His father, Izaak, and his mother, Jennie, already had five children. The Frenkils were prolific: Victor was the sixth, the newest in a line of children

who arrived just about every other year. Before long, the Frenkil children — Rose, Sam, Sophie, Ida, Celia, Victor, James, Sandy and Bernard — would resemble a mixed-gender baseball team.

The Frenkils lived in an older and eth-nically flavored neighborhood, just on the eastern edge

Victor's mother and father, Jennie and Izaak Frenkil, probably at the time of their engagement or marriage, circa 1897.

of downtown Baltimore. Victor's first home, at Baltimore and Exeter streets, sat in a densely populated neighborhood, a grid intersected by smaller courts and alleys, where many newly arrived immigrants sought to get their start in America. The streets Victor would know as a child were lined with brick houses built in the 1820s and 1830s. It was a district in which one group of people would settle, and, when they had pros-pered, would move on, perhaps to a larger new home not so close to factories, smoky rail yards, or so many immigrants.

And yet, the old locale seemed to have special meaning for Victor. Until the day he died, he kept his office only a few blocks away from where he was born.

The Baltimore where Victor Frenkil was born was a city

2

that beckoned European immigrants like the Frenkils and Goldscheiders (Jennie's parents), who left their native Austria to seek new lives in the United States. For Izaak Frenkil, it was a risk worth taking.

The Frenkil family was part of the steady migration from Europe. Each year thousands of Germans, Austrians, Poles and Russians flowed through Baltimore. In this period of flourishing immigration, one in four Baltimoreans spoke German as the mother tongue. Once settled in homes and jobs, they sent for those still living in the old country. So when Izaak and Jennie (her father, a teacher, arrived first; then her uncle, who studied medicine at Johns Hopkins) sailed to Baltimore, they had yet to meet.

In about a dozen years, Izaak Frenkil had acquired a solid, three-story home and built up a thriving business. He could even afford a servant to help his wife care for the house and nine children.

Izaak Frenkil was a self-made man, outspoken and driven. The fact that English was not his native language (he was a German-speaking Austrian) proved no obstacle. In his middle 20s when his first child was born, he was muscular and physically strong. He took chances in his business, and, according to a newspaper report in *The Sun* on 20 November 1912, he was accused of attempting to bribe the city plumbing inspector with $100. Undaunted, he hired a powerful, politically well connected lawyer to defend him. The case dragged on for three years, thanks to numerous postponements. There is no evidence that he was ever convicted. Years later Victor, like his father, would find himself in similar court battles.

Izaak, or "Ike" as he was known, was fascinated by construction, designing and building mechanical devices. Never afraid to roll up his sleeves and work, he had a good mind for figures.

Izaak Frenkil had come to the right city to make money. Baltimore had recently installed a new sewage system. Hundreds of streets were torn up. At the same time, homeowners were making the conversion to indoor plumbing. Izaak named his business the Baltimore Plumbing Supply Company.

He was ingenious (as his son Victor was to be). By 1920 he had a patent on an invention he called the Acme Frost Proof Closet. It was a piece of plumbing engineering of his own making, a commode to be used in industrial mills and schools that conserved water, designed to withstand the severest weather at a time when outdoor plumbing was commonplace. This complicated piece of engineering had 25 parts, each of which he detailed in his catalog. Izaak's delight in studying an engineering problem, then coming up with a solution for it, appealed to his son. Throughout his life Victor felt that, whatever the problem, he could study it, break it apart and reassemble it to suit his needs.

Ike and his workers made many of their plumbing parts on belt-driven machines. If he received extra large orders for plumbing parts, he expanded the

Brother James (on pony) and Victor at age 11 in front of the family home at 4312 Fernhill Avenue.

hours in his workday accordingly. He was not only willing to work hard, he seemed to enjoy it — another trait he passed on to Victor. He already owned a plant on Central Avenue in Baltimore (it had its own railroad siding), a second store on Maryland Avenue in North Baltimore and a branch each in Norfolk and Newport News, Virginia.

His work ethic notwithstanding, Izaak was a father who recognized his parental responsibilities. He had nine children to raise, and four sons to educate in the hard-knocks way of business. Most of all, he wanted them to succeed on their own.

He was an effective teacher. His busy shop became a trade school for his sons. His inventive side — his life-long habit of trying to make a device from parts or pieces in his factory — appealed to Victor, who also inherited his father's love of tinkering and working with his hands. In later years, when Ike lost a leg to diabetes, Victor rigged up a series of levers so he could drive a car.

"Ike was bright, dynamic and strict," said his son, James. "As his child, you did what he told you to do. He was not overbearing, but his word ruled. You obeyed him. He taught us all to work. He was born a poor boy who succeeded by his own labors." And, while he sold plumbing supplies, he always wore a diamond embellished gold ring, a ring later worn by his son and grandson.

Ike Frenkil's concept of what constituted a day's work would have put most people off. He was habitually at his business well before the sun rose. When his sons were old enough to be productive, they followed him to his business and were given tasks. They recall being hauled out of their warm and comfortable beds before sunrise. While Victor may have complained about getting up early as a child, he spent the rest of his life rising at the hour his father had. "He was not necessar-

Victor with his mother, Jennie, outside the family home, circa 1928.

Victor with two lady friends, about 16 years, dapper in bow tie and jacket.

ily a religious man, but we were all brought up to be honest," James Frenkil recalled many years later.

Recollections of Jennie Frenkil indicate that she led a conscientious domestic life, outfitting her home with tasteful wallpaper and gaslight chandeliers hung with crystal pendants. Of course, they had modern plumbing, probably a novelty in their neighborhood. She admitted to not being much of a cook, but still made sure there was plenty on the table.

The family got their butter, cheese and dairy products from a milk wagon that called at the house daily. The milk that was delivered in those days contained a high percentage of cream that floated at the top of the glass bottles. The young Frenkils developed a taste for this thick, rich cream and often competed over who would get the lion's share of the tasty stuff for their breakfast cereal. When the competition for the cream grew too intense, Jennie gave in and ordered a separate gill — about a half pint — for each of her brood. Victor never relinquished his affection for foods rich in butterfat.

The newly prosperous Frenkils were upwardly mobile in every sense of the word. Izaak owned a chestnut-colored horse named Charlie and a carriage. The nine children somehow managed to pile into the rig at the same time. Victor recalled watching Charlie pace throughout the city streets and enjoying the rhythmic clop-clop of his hooves. Some 70 years later, Victor delighted in arriving in a horse and carriage for the annual Flower Mart held each May at Mount Vernon Place.

Izaak Frenkil did not keep his family in an aging house in a neighborhood of newly arrived immigrants for long. For young families with the financial ability to move up the social ladder, the pull of the city's suburbs was strong. For Jews, who would not have been welcome in many parts of North and Northeast Baltimore, the obvious choice was Northwest

Baltimore, on the high ground adjacent to Druid Hill Park. The family initially moved to a home on Mondawmin Avenue, but did not stay there long. By 1913, after their last child, Bernard, was born, they settled at 4312 Fernhill Avenue, at the corner of Gwynn Oak Avenue, in West Arlington-Forest Park. It was a large, gracious residence surrounded by porches, trees and a backyard garden. Canvas awnings shaded the verandas. The roof had a widow's walk and there were large upstairs bedrooms where the children could play. This would be the home where the elder Frenkils would reside for the rest of their lives (Izaak died in 1936; Jennie lived until 1952).

Jennie, whose taste for a gracious home never diminished, kept a flower garden and outfitted 4312 Fernhill with velvet draperies, antique furniture and Oriental carpets. There were also a piano and weekly lessons for the children from a teacher, Miss Maude Stein. The younger Frenkil children did not like the regimen of the lessons, although their oldest sister, Rose, had talent for and interest in the piano. Victor and his sister, Celia, far preferred to put on roller skates and take off down the street when Miss Stein was due.

Family members recalled that Victor did, however, love music, and was an excellent dancer. "In the summer my parents took a house at Pen Mar Park at the Blue Ridge Summit," recalled James Frenkil. "There was a dance pavilion that looked over the valley. Victor was always musical. He liked to dance, and he liked the ladies."

Victor recalled many years later, "When I was in my seventies, I hired a piano teacher and learned how to play all over again. In a way, I'm surprised I wasn't interested as a child. When I was 12 years old, I began writing songs, and badgering my sister Sandy into sending them to publishers. I was bitterly disappointed every time the mail brought a rejection.

After all, Irving Berlin was already a huge success and he was only a few years older than I was."

Jennie also engaged a Hebrew teacher for her children so they could learn the language of her people. He came each week and the Frenkil children resisted, not wanting to take on more schoolwork. They recalled that, if they missed a verb, their teacher, a stern man with cold eyes, would rap them on their knuckles with a wooden ruler. "There we'd be, the nine Frenkil children sitting around the breakfast table, squirming and wiggling in our seats, trying to think of some way to skip out of the Hebrew lesson. But we did pick up a little Hebrew and in the process we learned something about the history of our people as well," Victor said.

Jennie Frenkil knew her limitations in the Fernhill Avenue kitchen, so she had a cook who prepared the main meals. The girls were expected to help so they could become the cook their mother never was.

As Celia said, "Mother wasn't much of a cook. Sometimes she would get the urge to bake, but her bread was like a loaf of lead. About the only thing she could fix was chicken soup. But we worked closely with the cook who knew what she was doing. We learned from the cook."

Sister Sophie later laughed about her training in the kitchen where 11 people sat down to eat at the same time. "It was like cooking for a restaurant. When I married my husband, Lee, and prepared our first dinner, I cooked up two pounds of rice. It took me a long time to adjust to meals for just two."

The Frenkil boys enjoyed a lively childhood. For mischief, they sometimes rigged up a string across the streetcar tracks that ran alongside their parents' home. At night, minutes before a trolley car was due to pass, they'd drape a newspaper over the string. In the dim night light, the car's operator saw what he thought was an obstruction on the tracks and would hit the noisy air brakes, causing giggles among the hiding Frenkil children.

Victor and James Frenkil also engaged in another activity, that of selling subscriptions to *The Baltimore News*. James, the younger of the two sons, would ring a doorbell. Because he was so young and so charming, he could frequently win a few minutes listening time from the prospective subscriber. After James warmed up the target to the point of receiving signs of encouragement, Victor would pop out and clinch the customer with an order blank. The boys won many prizes for their salesmanship: an express wagon, pairs of skates and other premiums. "I'd follow Victor around. I was pretty tenacious. We were very blessed as a good, solid family," James Frenkil said. "We enjoyed each other's company."

Victor told a pair of stories about his youth. One concerned the bluebells that came up in the open fields near his home. He discovered that he could make money by cajoling his brothers and sisters to pick them for him, paying them three cents a bunch. He then sold the crop to a local flower seller, and eventually wound up with a tidy profit of $20. He had sent out his siblings over and over again, all the while urging them to pick larger bunches. Even though he wound up losing the money (he put it in the cellar and it mysteriously disappeared), he loved the idea of a business plan that worked, organizing others to perform duties that made him money.

Not all his childhood antics worked so well. A neighborhood ice cream parlor owner bet him his $3 weekly allowance that he couldn't eat five chocolate sundaes at one sitting. Victor took the bet — and in fact could not down the fifth sundae. He lost the money, then later realized the sundaes were double-sized. He vowed never to let anyone get the better of him.

The ice-cream incident, he said, proved a valuable lesson. When taking a risk, do everything you can to put the odds in your favor.

VICTOR FRENKIL'S HIGH SCHOOL YEARS

A short walk from the Frenkil home was Forest Park High School, an institution that opened its doors in the fall of 1924. It was here that Victor would spend the best part of the next five years. He was a member of the first class to enroll at the school. When he graduated in the class of February 1929 (he had taken some time off to work for his father in 1927), he behaved as if Forest Park High School had been built with him and his needs in mind.

"Victor was dyslexic and he didn't know how to study," said his brother, James. "He got through Forest Park on the strength of his personality. He developed it so exquisitely. All the teachers were very fond of him. I'd see him walk down the hall and into the principal's office as if he owned the place. And yet I don't think he ever opened a book to study."

Victor's graduation photo from Forest Park High School, Class of February 1929.

An account in his yearbook, the "Forester", gives an idea of his busy and happy years there: "Vic Frenkil is undoubtedly the most versatile member of the senior class. He has successfully attempted about everything the school has to offer. His athletics are quite outstanding for he had played both basketball and soccer and was elected captain of the track team."

His entry in the book goes on to note that he was the South Atlantic Champion for the quarter mile run, a record he proudly held for almost twenty years (it was finally broken in 1946). The medal he won was one of his cherished possessions.

He had the medal mounted on a stand and often showed it to guests in his office. He would tell them that he set the record running in a shoe with a defective heel. His brother James recalled that "A lot of his accomplishments were based on brain power and the will to win, rather than on his muscle power." At the age of 17, Victor had already been exhibiting a personal characteristic that over his lifetime would

Victor dressed to run, a sport at which he not only excelled, but in which he held the high-school record for many years.

develop in so many ways: he liked a challenge and loved mastering it. He may not have been a born athlete — his brother said he did not train or practice much for his big race — yet he acted as if he were going to win. He fixed his eye on the prize and willed his way to the finish line ahead of the competition.

Victor (on the right) with two of his pals outside a Forest Park High School classroom, about 16 years of age.

Victor was vice-president of his sophomore class, president of his junior class and vice-president of his senior class, and was voted "the most versatile". He joined school clubs, including the Craftsmen's Club and the Radio Club, and worked on school dances and operettas. He was chairman of the ring committee. His salesmanship was evident as the yearbook's business manager: His year's edition had many more advertisements than earlier ones. His yearbook entry ended on a prophetic note: "We are told that he intends to enter the business world".

The fact he was elected to class presidencies speaks not only of his leadership skills, but also of his popularity among his peers. He was a well-known personality in a coeducational school of more than 1,000 pupils. The large number of local businesses that purchased space in the yearbook is testimony to his pleasure at selling a product and convincing prospective advertisers of its merits.

When a committee formed to celebrate Forest Park's fiftieth anniversary in 1975, its members designated Victor Frenkil as their "best-known alumnus". For decades he funded a pair of scholarships. One was in the name of the school's athletic director, Rex Sims, with whom he had cultivated a lasting friendship; the other scholarship was in his own name.

While at Forest Park, Victor developed a characteristic he would display throughout his life. While most students would retain a certain distance from the authorities such as the principal, Victor treated the school's head administrator as if he were an old friend. Victor had such a good relationship with Glenn Owens, the Forest Park principal, that he could walk into his office without an appointment. He offered the principal rides in his car and sought his advice. He called him frequently and enjoyed access to the principal's thoughts and good graces. Victor found early on that the ability to initiate and maintain the friendship of those in high places served him better in life than a knowledge of history or physics.

In the academic department, Victor was a failure. His entry in the high-school yearbook

In 1956 Victor received an honorary diploma from Forest Park, which read: "As the member of our class who has most distinguished himself in business and civic affairs. In tribute we are proud of that which he gained from our school and his unselfish efforts to further the cause of justice and charity to his fellow man." On his right is Vic's mentor, Ruth Kramer.

14

did not mention his grades. He was, in fact, not a scholar. As a child he had trouble reading books (it was said he never read more than four or five books in his entire life). He had a learning disability known today as dyslexia. Left-handed, his handwriting was atrocious, essentially illegible. In that era, students were trained in the art of penmanship. Ideally, their handwriting was supposed to bend to the right. Victor's did not. His father worked with him to improve his writing. He finally offered him a reward of $5 if he could fill a composition notebook with legible handwriting. Victor tried repeatedly, then had his sister help him out. In the end, his father seemed satisfied with the effort although, to the end of his life, Victor's signature was a distorted, illegible scribble.

He might have failed to make it through school had it not been for the helpful intervention of one very special teacher. She was Ruth Kramer, who taught physics and was the senior class advisor. She took a liking to Victor, seeing something in him he didn't see in himself. She began helping him with all his homework. She was patient and had a way of explaining subjects. She showed him ways of understanding subjects he had never previously grasped because of his dyslexia. Victor dazzled her with his charms and showered her with attention. Though there are no records of any behind-the-scenes assistance, it would be logical to assume that she implored school authorities to let him pass. She knew he was not trying to duck schoolwork. She observed that he was intelligent, but his studying failed to get him the grades of other students. The 1929 yearbook was dedicated to her, an honor that Victor no doubt influenced.

Victor never forgot her help. Years later, in the 1960s, Ruth was living with a brother and two sisters on 25th Street, when one brother suddenly died and, the next day, a sister died. So he took her under wing. He arranged to have her and her other sister, Helen, moved to the Marylander Apartments, where he resided. Many evenings they joined the Frenkil table for supper, 40 years after Ruth's former pupil received a diploma.

Victor should have graduated in 1928. Instead, he was a member of the January 1929 graduating class because he took some time off to work for his father, who needed his help and realized that Victor had all the instincts of a competent businessman. As a 17-year-old high-school junior, he had already learned the plumbing supply business and could repair anything around the house that was broken. Now his father wanted him to supervise a huge contract he had inherited.

"My father was a pretty wise man," said James Frenkil. "He recognized Victor's independent side and wanted to play to it. Victor liked his father's challenge."

A Maryland plumbing company had contracted to build the sewer system for Rock Creek Park in Washington, D.C., a large and potentially lucrative project. Izaak Frenkil had provided the bonding for the job. For a fee, he guaranteed that the sewer would be completed. The Maryland contractor walked away from the project, and Izaak had to make good and complete the job himself.

Ike called Victor into his office and said: "You take over the project. You drop out of school, go down to Washington and make sure everything's done right and on time. OK?"

Victor paused for a moment. It would be rough work and he wanted to make certain it was worth the effort. For a long time he had wanted his own car, but cars cost more money than he was likely to earn in the foreseeable future. But knowing this contract was worth a lot to his father, he decided to make an outrageous demand.

"I'll do it," he said, "if you buy me a brand new Chevrolet."

16

Izaak fumed, but recognized how much he needed his son, so he bought Victor the car. Oddly enough, Victor was not much of a driver, and for most of his life had someone else drive for him. He persuaded a high-school friend and class officer named Nelson Fenimore to join him in the venture. They rented an apartment in Silver Spring. They had their freedom, but the work was hard.

As foreman, Victor faced problems and responsibilities. The site was hilly; a five-horse team pulled a large wooden sled full of sand, gravel and cement so a crew could construct a foot-thick sewer. They were doing the job according to specifications until a nosy building inspector threw his weight around.

"I want you to add another bag of concrete to the mix," he told Victor.

"But the specifications call for doing just what we're doing," Victor responded.

"Do what I say anyway," the inspector replied.

Just then the inspector caught sight of Victor's new Chevrolet. He walked over, poked his head inside, and rubbed the leather seat. "This is a beautiful car," he said.

An idea came to Victor, who asked, "Would you like to take it for a ride?" The inspector smiled broadly and Victor tossed him the keys. The inspector took off and drove around the countryside. It was the last time Victor had any trouble from him.

Years later, Victor recalled an incident that occurred in suburban Washington. While driving to work one morning, he and Nelson saw two attractive girls standing by a car on the side of the road. They had a flat tire. The boys stopped and offered to help. Instead of taking the flat tire to a filling station, they put on the spare from the Chevrolet, took the girls' telephone numbers and told them they would pick up the tire that evening.

"We'll be at the camp meeting on the outside of town," they said. "Why not meet us there."

Victor and Nelson thought they had run across a pair of attractive and potentially accommodating girls. So they showed up at the "camp meeting" that evening full of expectations, only to discover they had been invited to a Methodist revival. Before they could turn around, the girls led them to a tent where they sat down on hard wooden benches. Soon the assembly was shouting "Amen" and "Hallelujah".

Nothing like this had ever happened in a synagogue. Nelson pointed over to a tree, where the girls had left the spare tire. Victor nodded and they both jumped up, grabbed the tire and ran as fast as they could. The girls probably didn't even notice that the boys had left.

The Frenkils were Jews who respected their faith. Saturday, which was payday on the job, was the Sabbath. Victor would, by ancient custom, have to walk rather than drive his car. So he walked the several miles to the work site, swinging the payroll sack as if it were full of peanuts, rather than $3,500 in wages.

The Rock Creek sewer was installed on time. Izaak was aware that his son had done a man's job. And Victor had taken an important first step in what would become his life's work.

II. Unbounded Ambition

"Ambition is an uncomfortable companion many times. He creates a discontent with present surroundings and achievements; he is never satisfied but always pressing forward to better things in the future. Restless, energetic, purposeful, it is ambition that makes of the creature a real man."

Lyndon Baines Johnson

Victor Frenkil wanted to go to college. He had graduated from Forest Park with a C-minus average, poor study habits and all the charm he could muster. In fact, it was only through the intervention of sympathetic high-school teachers that he emerged with a diploma.

In the late winter of 1929, when many of his classmates were signing up for college, Victor set his eye on Hopkins, the prestigious school where his younger brother James would later enroll. It had the toughest academic standards in the state. Victor's school friends were not encouraging. Most believed he'd never gain admission. But Victor loved a challenge, so against all odds, he applied. Then, through a series of events he would talk about for years, he found himself admitted to the state's most academically difficult institution, Johns Hopkins University.

Victor arrived at the registrar's office one day with no

19

appointment. On the strengths of his personality, and his ability to talk his way past a secretary, he got in the door to see Roland P. Dempsey, Hopkins' registrar. The meeting was brief because Dempsey had his hat on and was about to rush home — his wife had called to say his gutters and downspouts were overflowing and something had to be done immediately.

Victor saw a window of opportunity. His years working at his father's business had taught him a lot about home maintenance.

"Let me go with you," Victor suggested. "I know all about plumbing. I can help you fix the leak."

When the two arrived at the house, Victor saw what needed to be done. "We're going to need a five-inch gutter, a couple of four-inch downspouts, shanks and circles." He and the registrar went to the local hardware store and bought the supplies, which Victor then installed. In a few hours, Victor was seated in the much-relieved registrar's office. They discussed Victor's years at Forest Park and got around to the touchy subject of his grades. "You are obviously bright," the registrar said. "You have common sense, which is probably more valuable in the real world than book sense. We can test you. If you do well, we'll overlook the grades and give you a chance."

Victor thanked him and left, assuming that a letter would arrive, scheduling the entrance examination. When a letter from Hopkins did arrive, it was one congratulating him on being accepted into its freshman class.

Victor duly enrolled, but soon found that all the problems he encountered at Forest Park had not only followed him to Hopkins, but, given the unusually high standards there, were even worse. Hopkins was not for him, he decided, and dropped out.

Victor's father, Izaak, was not through overseeing the practical education of his sons just yet. He was well aware of a rivalry between his oldest son, Samuel, and Victor, both of whom were competitors within the family and his plumbing business, where each had worked.

While a student at Forest Park, Victor had befriended the school's shop teacher, William "Bill" Jolly. The two even formed a home-improvement company, Jolly Construction, and worked jobs in the neighborhood. This initiative impressed Izaak.

By 1930 Izaak's health was deteriorating. In a few years, he would lose a leg. (In fact, he did not have long to live after that — he died in 1936.) He was making preparations for his sons to take over his

Victor's parents, Jennie and Izaak, in their later years. Vic tended to favor his father.

interests. Sam, the older of the two, was brought into the family wholesale plumbing-supply business. Victor was set up in a new company, a roofing and sheet-metal company called Bethlehem Sheet Metal.

Victor lost no time. He needed a good location downtown and selected the estate of Joe Gans, the African-American former lightweight champion of the world, who died in 1910. With the winnings made from his many and celebrated prize fights, he had purchased this property and opened the Goldfield hotel. It was now owned by his widow, who was living outside Keyser, West Virginia.

An ordinary mortal would have taken the easier route of looking for another location. Not Victor. He'd made his decision and traveled to Keyser, where his initial inquiries about Margaret Gans, the boxer's widow, were met with blank stares. He was told to ask a farmer who came into town once a week to pick up hay. After locating the farmer, who said he knew where Mrs. Gans lived, Victor hitched a wagon ride. It took about four hours to reach her home, an old wooden house that leaned to one side. When he arrived, he found an old woman sitting on the front porch. She was smoking a pipe.

Victor made his pitch with the usual charm, masking his preparation (he had come with a lease in his pocket). "How much do you want to pay me?" she asked. "A hundred dollars a year", he replied. She signed the lease and Victor paid her for what he felt would be a promising business location.

Back in Baltimore, Victor addressed his enterprise with his customary enthusiasm. Izaak watched as his sons took over for him. He soon retired from the day-to-day operations. After the stock market crash of 1929, construction (as most businesses) slowed. But, to make matters worse, the two brothers, Sam and Victor, were locked in a dispute. Sam, and his general manager, Oscar Loeb, charged that Victor had become a competitor to the family's wholesale plumbing-supply business. They claimed his company was actually a subsidiary of their own. To prove their point — infuriating Victor in the process — Sam and the general manager entered the old Goldfield Hotel and confiscated Victor's account books. With access to his records, they now called his suppliers and somehow persuaded them to cut off his credit.

At that time Victor had a large order pending with Continental Roofing Mills in East Baltimore. If he failed to deliver the goods, he would be in trouble with his customers. Just as he had visited the Hopkins registrar, he went to see Continental's president, Stanley Woodward. Victor arrived in overalls and told his tale. Mr. Woodward looked him over and said, "You look like a good honest boy, I'll send you two cars of roofing".

Victor was able to survive for three or four months, all the while his brother and Oscar Loeb continued to place obstacles in his path. Victor ultimately decided it would be best to sell the company. He located a buyer, Kahl Brothers, a well-known sheet-metal firm in the same neighborhood.

But even this did not end the family dispute. Sam went to his mother and said Victor was trying to steal from his own family. She was disturbed by the charges. Victor, in turn, sought counsel from his father's best friend, Mano Schwartz.

"What should I do?" he asked Mr. Schwartz, who responded, "If you are fighting with your mother, then you should give them the key".

Victor initially did not react well to the suggestion. He had worked hard to get his business started. Besides, Bethlehem Sheet Metal was just beginning to make a profit. Victor felt his brother was merely trying to eliminate a tough competitor. He also knew that his brother was giving a one-sided version of the story to his mother.

They agreed to a compromise. The two brothers, along with Sam's manager, Oscar Loeb, and a representative of Kahl Brothers, would meet in the office of attorney Harry Levin, who would act as arbitrator. Levin would hear both sides and render a decision, which would be binding on both parties. Levin sided with brother Sam and Loeb. They sold Victor's company to Kahl for $12,000; Victor got nothing for his efforts. As it turned out, the sheet-metal business flourished for another 15 years until Mr. Kahl died.

The incident alienated the two brothers for a number of years. Although they would later reconcile, the family dispute hit Victor in a vulnerable area. He was humiliated. He had put in long hours, made prudent decisions, satisfied his customers — and lost everything. He learned a lesson: the next time, he would be tougher. Working hard was one thing, but working hard and smart was another. At 23, he resolved to do things differently.

Victor gave Johns Hopkins one more try. He went back to college, only to encounter trouble with his old nemesis, mathematics, which he was soon in danger of failing. For $2 an hour, he hired a classmate named Hawkins as a tutor. One evening, after Victor had completed his lesson in his tutor's dorm room, Hawkins said he could not find his wallet.

Victor with the woman he would marry, Margaret Panzer, in a professional photo taken in 1931.

He reported Victor to Hopkins officials, claiming he had made off with his billfold. The next day, Victor, who had no knowledge of the alleged theft, was called into the dean's office. Accusations flew back and forth. A police officer was called. Victor was so outraged by the situation that a scuffle broke out. The dean and another police officer restrained him. Victor ultimately hired a private detective to prove his innocence. Then, some weeks later, Hawkins used his library card, a card he had reported as lost in his wallet. It seems the wallet was not really lost after all. The incident so soured Victor on school that he dropped out again, this time for good.

Even without the wallet incident, it is highly unlikely that he would have made it through graduation at Johns Hopkins. He did not like to read or, more likely, did not want to read because his learning disability made it futile. For the rest of his life he would remain a non-reader, doing little more than skimming newspaper headlines to sniff out opportunity, or to find out who of importance was doing what to whom.

Yet his lack of formal education would not hold him back. Victor had a healthy dose of "street smarts" that made him far wiser and faster than most of his more educated colleagues. He also had a curious mind that worked overtime finding and solving problems and, of course, he loved a challenge. While remarkably intelligent in many ways, he simply was not cut out for academic endeavors, which he no doubt found boring rather than challenging.

One of the more serious challenges that he faced occurred in 1924, when he encountered a 15-year-old girl named Margaret Panzer, a bright, alert, attractive secretary who worked for a company that did payroll for his father. Vic noticed her when he would go by to pick up the payroll. He couldn't help but stare as he passed by. Like Victor, she was a willing, determined worker. She had recently left business school to take a job to help her mother keep the family together (her father had died in the influenza epidemic of 1918).

The Panzer and Frenkil families were dramatically different, yet had much in common. A good deal of German would have been spoken at her home because both her mother and father had ties to the old country. They worked in a family business: Several of her uncles made condiments and pickles that were sold in local markets. Margaret resided on Bank Street in Baltimore, not far from Victor's birthplace. She was a graduate of Saint Michael's School and attended the Baltimore College of Commerce, but dropped out to work. She had a ready smile and temperament that appealed to Victor.

Victor and Margaret dated for several years, often on the sly, because their parents were not happy with the relationship. Margaret's Roman-Catholic mother had trouble accepting a Jew as a possible son-in-law. The elder Frenkils were dubious of a prospective Christian daughter-in-law. She had even taken a new job at the John Knipp furniture and decorating company as a way to distance herself from the disapproving elders.

True to form, Victor grew more determined in his courting as the parents posed questions and offered objections. After many discussions, the final obstacle was overcome when Margaret agreed that any children she might have with Victor would follow their father's religion and cultural heritage. Victor agreed he would help support Margaret's mother.

With the marriage approved (or at least reluctantly accepted), Margaret selected her birthday as her wedding day. They were married on 15 February 1932, in the rectory of her home church, St. Michael's. The wedding was small, with only the priest and a witness present.

III.
GETTING STARTED

"The heavens are as deep as our aspirations are high."
Henry David Thoreau

Just around the corner from Keith's Theatre, where Park Avenue meets Lexington Street, was a building with a sign that read, "Baltimore Contractors". Three flights up, over a dentist's office, was the first office Victor Frenkil occupied.

He had just turned 23 and, with his youthful enthusiasm, could scarcely have picked a less auspicious beginning for the start of his business venture. He founded Baltimore Contractors in December of 1931, in the darkened days of the American depression.

That was not enough to discourage Victor, let alone stop him. He charged ahead, convinced there were always people with money to spend improving their offices and homes. When times are tough and business slows, shopkeepers can devote time to other activities, such as remodeling their stores, even if they have to do it on the cheap. Apartments and houses always need new roofs and porches.

As always, Victor was driven — a man who did not understand the meaning of the word "no". Much like his father, he slept very little, preferring to get to his office before daybreak.

He didn't drive to work; he'd often wave down a friend — or stranger — for a lift. Sometimes he walked, meeting people and striking up conversations. And he lived on the telephone. One classic photograph of him shows him engaged in conversation, with the phone to his ear. And, of course, he's the one doing the talking.

Victor seemed to thrive on what others saw as adversity. He found opportunity where others saw only failure. The more difficult the conditions, the faster and more accurately his mind worked to turn them in his favor.

He found it easy to overlook the fact that his financial assets were meager. When he started his company, he had no more than a wedding gift from his parents, a nest egg of $300. It was minimal, even for a small business. The name he chose reflected the aspirations of the man: "Baltimore Contractors". There was an inherent implication that the whole city was his client (as indeed much of it would come to be).

The entire staff consisted of Victor and Margaret, who was still working for a furniture and decorating company. As jobs came in, Victor would hire the people necessary to complete them.

Never afraid to think big, Victor chose to spend half the money he had on advertising. He paid a man a dollar a day to walk the streets inside a sandwich sign and pass out printed leaflets touting his services. He also put an advertisement in the local newspapers. The type was so small that it almost required a magnifying glass to read it:

A GOOD JOB AT A FAIR PRICE
Baltimore Contractors, Specialists in Home Improvement
- Painting, Papering, Flooring, Roofing
- Remodeling Store Fronts, Factories, Homes, Garages

- Concrete Block, Brick, Frame
- Heating and Plumbing: Steam, Hot Water, Oil
- Free Estimates, Free Blue Prints Cheerfully Given Day or Night
- No Deposit, Easy Terms, Begin to Pay July

> Baltimore Contractors
> 210 Park Avenue Plaza 8399,
> Night phone Lib. 5610

The advertisement was remarkably well done for someone with no experience in the craft. What is interesting is how it reflects the character of the man himself. He offered "a good job at a fair price", which was his personal, philosophic approach to business. Then,

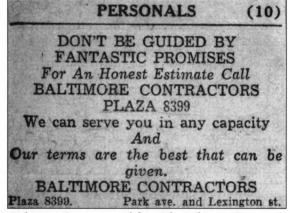

Baltimore Contractors ad from The Baltimore Sun, Wednesday, 30 November 1932. Size: 2" x 1.5".

ever ambitious, he stretched things a bit by suggesting experience in almost every area of remodeling, from painting and papering to heating and plumbing.

It was a gamble. But Victor and Margaret had to start somewhere. Baltimore Contractors took small jobs and allowed its customers to pay later. The company did not even require deposits. Anything to jumpstart the business.

What separated Victor from most people was his indomitable personality, his ability to transform difficulty into opportunity. When business was slow, he would ring doorbells in the neighborhood, introducing himself with a sincere smile and offering the services he had ballyhooed in his first advertisement. He made the sales pitch, asking questions, finding out what his potential customers might need, then trying to convince them that the most important thing at that moment was a new shop front or bathroom.

Times were tough. Even with Victor's natural ability to sell, it was still difficult to land work. He bid whatever he thought the market would bear. His ideal formula for bidding was to total the costs of the materials and labor and double it. With very little experience, it was difficult to estimate precisely how long a job would take, which often led to costly mistakes. As a result, he lost money on some jobs. Nevertheless, after his first year as a general contractor, the profit outweighed the loss. In the midst of the Great Depression, Baltimore Contractors got off to a successful start.

Victor's first contract was for a job at 716 N. Eden Street in East Baltimore. His bid: $25. The materials cost $6. The labor ran $4. Victor made $15, for a gross profit margin of 60 percent. Not bad for a beginner. That same year he painted the interior of a popcorn store and collected $5. His largest job for 1931 was an impressive $5,747 for redoing a large apartment in Roland Park.

Many decades later, his younger brother James recalled, "He made a success of the business on very little money. He knew how to work hard and kept at it".

Baltimore Contractors' books for those early years were recorded in Margaret's precise and meticulous hand. She kept them in a three-ring notebook whose cover was decorated with drawings of college football players and coeds.

Two years later, in 1933, Victor's ads took a new and different tack, one that reflected a change in the company's direction. Baltimore Contractors now advertised itself as having "30 years' experience" in the construction business. Victor had hired his first full-time, non-family employee, John T. "Pop" Croswell, who had just been laid off by Morrow Brothers, a large general contractor where he had worked for the previous 28 years.

Victor would often recall that day. It was October of 1932; there was a chilly wind blowing outside. The onset of winter always slowed the construction business. Some outside work was simply impossible to do in freezing temperatures.

Victor remembered sitting in his

"Pop" Croswell, one of Victor's first (and most important) hires at Baltimore Contractors.

office, waiting for the phone to ring. He heard slow, deliberate steps on the staircase. When he opened the door, he found an elderly man with protruding ears. The man was dressed in faded overalls and old shoes.

Victor offered him a chair and asked, "What can I do for you?"

"I have to have a job," the man replied, without giving his name.

31

"And you want me to hire you?"

He nodded.

"Why should I do that?"

What followed was the story of a 73-year-old man who had been told by his boss that he was too old to work anymore.

Victor's first brush with celebrity (in the early 1930s): remodeling H. L. Mencken's bathroom, a job worth $800.

Victor listened and made his own assessment of him. The man may have been 73, but he had just climbed the three flights of stairs that led to the office. The fact that he was there at all, asking for work, demonstrated determination. And he didn't, in fact, look his age.

"What can you do?" Victor asked.

"I'm an estimator," the man said. He then listed all the major jobs he had estimated, which included banks, libraries, office buildings and factories.

Less astute people would likely have shown the man to the door and thanked him for his inquiry. On the surface, it seemed illogical to hire a new man as winter drew near, particularly one at such an advanced age.

Victor had no intention of devoting the rest of his life to painting popcorn shops and fixing bathrooms. He wanted bigger, more important jobs that would pay for the growth he dreamed of. He also knew, all too well, that in the months he had been running the company, his chief weakness had been in estimating the cost of a job. Victor was just too inexperienced to predict accurately the time it would take to complete a major project, the kind of job he wanted.

"Pop" Croswell was from an Eastern Shore family. As a young man, he'd been a carpenter's apprentice. He later took correspondence courses in mechanical drawing and mathematics. In the 1890s, he helped construct the Bauernschmidt Brewery and bottling house on Gay Street in Northeast Baltimore, and installed one of the first mechanical ice-making plants in the city. He also helped build the Fifth Regiment Armory, three Enoch Pratt Free Library buildings and several banks.

He was particularly proud of his work on the beautifully carved and crafted Christmas tower, a Gothic-style gray stone addition to Emmanuel Episcopal Church at Cathedral and Read streets.

Victor sat and stared at him for a moment. He needed someone with these qualifications. The man seemed to have just what he wanted. Why not make the jump right now? Victor, who almost always trusted his instincts, hired John "Pop" Croswell on the spot.

It turned out to be one of the smartest moves Victor made. Croswell proved to be the best estimator Victor ever had. From that day on, the company picked up momentum and began to land more substantial work. Croswell remained with Victor for the next 18 years, often working nine-hour days. He lived to be 91.

In December of 1932, two months after Victor had hired "Pop" Croswell, Margaret gave birth to their first child, a daughter named Janet, named for Janet Gaynor, the first actress to win an Oscar at the Academy Awards (who, as a mat-

The first home Victor and Margaret owned, at Park Heights Avenue and Trainor Road.

ter of curiosity, was born "Laura Gainor"). In those days, women spent two weeks in the hospital following the birth of a child, so Margaret would miss Christmas at home. Victor, whose religious observance did not include Christmas, sensed Margaret's feelings. Each day, as he went to visit her at the hospital, he walked past a decorated evergreen tree in the lobby. No one noticed that he pinched an ornament as he passed and brought the glass decoration to her room. By the end of her stay, the room was filled with little bells, trumpets and Christmas balls.

Shortly after Margaret returned home, she reviewed Baltimore Contractors' books. In that first year, Victor had sold $20,000 worth of home improvements. Of that amount, some $5,000 was profit, an amazingly successful figure for a young company getting started in the middle of the greatest economic depression the country had faced.

The happy couple now entertained thoughts about buying their own home. There was money to hire someone to answer the phones and keep the books. Victor found a three-story frame house on Park Heights Avenue. It was large; too large in fact. But it had three floors, the lower two of which could be rented as apartments. The rent would pay the mortgage. He also negotiated so that the two vacant lots next door would be part of the purchase.

The Frenkils bought their home on 24 February 1933. Fortunately, Victor had brought a certified check to seal the $6,250 deal: the country was in such financial upheaval that the banks were closed the next day. The young family took possession of the house and moved into the third floor, from which Victor gazed at the two adjoining vacant lots, wondering what opportunity they might present.

Years later he liked to tell the story of what happened one winter in the middle 1930s after he had secured the lots that adjoined his home so that he could build four pairs of semi-detached stone houses, putting two on Park Heights Avenue and two on Trainor Road. While excavating the sloping site, he uncovered a boulder that par-

Two of the four houses Victor built next to his home on Park Heights Avenue, approximately 1940.

tially filled the otherwise empty lot. He didn't want the expense of hiring a crane or steam shovel to remove it, so he put one of his best workers on the job, a bricklayer from Northeast Baltimore named Charles DeGraw. Victor always said Degraw could do the job of any two men when he was working and not downing a few at the local tavern. On a cold March afternoon, while waiting for Charlie and his men to come back and lay foundation brick for the homes, Victor decided to build a fire to ease the cold. He took some lumber scraps and lighted them just alongside the rock. The fire burned throughout the afternoon.

The work crew never showed up. As it grew dark, Victor decided to douse the fire with a garden hose. He was not aware of it, but the flames had heated the rock to such a temperature that, when he turned on the ice-cold water, the rock shattered. He now had piles of smaller rocks that could be easily hauled away or reused in the foundation. Victor often used this story to show how an apparently negative situation can sometimes be turned to one's advantage.

In a few months, Victor needed to sell the completed houses to recoup his investment. He decided on a price of $7,777, a figure he picked because it was associated with good luck, a "lucky seven". Victor relished the construction problems of the second set of houses. The land dipped down in the rear, making access to the homes' garages difficult. Victor thought about the problem, then came up with a way to engineer the driveway. He then had a brochure printed, listing 77 reasons why these homes were worth buying. They sold in a couple of weeks.

Victor's inventive mind served him well during a family emergency. After his father, Izaak, lost his leg (amputated due to a severe blood clot), he was also depressed by financial problems, since the hard economic times had cut into his plumbing supply business. Victor, his brothers and sisters suggested that their father hire a chauffeur to drive him around. He refused.

Neither man surrendered easily to adversity. Victor reasoned that, if his father still had the use of one leg and both hands, there was no reason why a car could not be outfitted with controls. Now the two family inventors, Victor and Izaak, put their heads together. They devised a bar connected to the brake and clutch that allowed the driver to operate with one good leg and an artificial limb that Izaak had had fitted. Izaak drove again and lived for another three years.

Sometime in 1935 Victor's business outgrew its first home at Lexington Avenue and Park Street. In a curious, and telling move, he relocated it back to the old neighborhood where he learned the business from his father — and where he first encountered Margaret.

Victor then rented a vacant building next door to his father's old Central Avenue plumbing business. And, for the remainder of his own life, Victor's business headquarters would remain several blocks away, always on the same East Baltimore Street where his father had operated.

As 1934 came to an end, Margaret and Victor came to a decision about the holidays. They would celebrate Christmas after all, complete with presents and decorations. After all, it would be Janet's third Christmas. Would there be a tree in the house? Victor spoke with his old high-school principal, Glenn Owens, with whom he maintained a friendship. "Christmas is a joyous occasion," the educator told him. Victor replied he wanted his child to be proud she was Jewish. "Many who celebrate Christmas are non-Christians," Owens explained, "simply embracing the universal principles of peace, giving and

Victor and Margaret at a party at the Belvedere Hotel in the mid-1940s.

good will. It's as much an American tradition as it is a religious one." Thus, a custom was born. The Frenkils would be a Jewish family who had a Christmas tree — as well as a party for the employees at Baltimore Contractors. These annual gatherings started small. But, by 1938, seven years after the business began, the Christmas party filled the ballroom of a downtown hotel.

At the time of their marriage, Margaret (with, no doubt, a little gentle persuasion from Victor) agreed that their children would be raised in the Jewish religion. This, of course, violated the dictates of Roman Catholicism, which insist that children of Catholics be baptized in that faith. Margaret, while thoroughly Catholic, was by nature not a zealot. Nevertheless, from the point of view of the Church, this meant that she was no longer a member in good standing. Given this formal rejection, along with her deference to her husband, her decision to honor her agreement (and probably because Margaret did not like conflict), she ceased attending Sunday mass. She felt abandoned unreasonably by the Catholic Church, but, since the strict doctrine gave her no alternative, was comfortable with the decision.

She remained close to her mother, a pious Catholic who attended mass daily (and must have lit more than a few candles to protect her errant daughter). Margaret was also faithful to her brother, a Marianist brother (a German order of the Catholic Church) who taught philosophy and was a dean at the University of Dayton. He, too, understanding her dilemma, must have used whatever influence he had with the Almighty to help keep her in a blessed state.

Margaret wanted a happy family life, and if that meant suppressing her own faith in favor of her husband's, that was a sacrifice she was willing to make.

Many years later she returned to the Church, largely through the efforts of a priest named Father William Au, a kind, understanding, liberal cleric who became a good friend of the family. She was succumbing to Alzheimer's disease and, realizing what was happening to her, yearned for the faith that had been comforting to her as a child. Victor, sadly aware of her deteriorating condition, went to two friends for help. One was William Keeler, Cardinal of Baltimore. The other was Victor's lawyer, George McManus, well known in the local Catholic community.

Cardinal Keeler called Father Au and asked him to visit

Margaret, which he did — with great frequency. Father Au remembers how clearly she remembered the litany, and, in spite of the disease, could recite many different prayers with him. He was impressed with her honesty, her acceptance of her faith and her great sense of dignity,

This great kindness on the part of Father Au was later repaid in the form of a significant philanthropic gift to his parish by Victor and Margaret's older son, also named Victor (but called "Bruz" by many), and his wife, Nancy.

Much of Victor's business success came because of his skills with people. He was a charmer, one who had the time to listen, to demonstrate genuine personal interest in others and forge personal ties. He recalled two jobs from the days of the many rebuilt back porches and remodeled bathrooms. He had been hired by the manager of McCrory's Five and Ten Store, which was involved in a lawsuit. A customer said she had slipped and injured her back after falling on the store's linoleum-covered staircase.

McCrory's lawyer hired Victor to disassemble the stairs, treads and all, and bring the pieces to the courtroom for re-assembly. The lawyer was smart, and knew that his case would be stronger were he able to visualize for the jury what had happened and why. Victor's crew took the stairs apart and rebuilt them at the Court House. The case was argued and the jury came back with a verdict in favor of McCrory's. Victor submitted a bill for $370, which was returned with a check for $800. The lawyer was delighted with the work.

The second job Vic liked to remember came in the middle 1930s, one that appeared to be routine, but turned out to have lasting positive repercussions. He got a call to refinish a basement clubroom in the neighborhood of Guilford. He visited the home on Suffolk Road and quoted a price to its owner, a

Baltimore Contractors' annual summer picnic, 1950. Shown are Margaret, Bebe (standing), Janet and, to her left, Frenkil biographer-to-be Tony Weir.

Mr. Charles F. Brown. Baltimore Contractors finished the job on time and on budget, and Mr. Brown expressed his satisfaction.

Victor did not realize it, but his customer was in fact the president of the Western Maryland Railway, then a large transportation company headquartered in downtown Baltimore. Three years later, the company asked for bids for the removal of a decaying terra cotta cornice on the roof of their Fidelity Warehouse in the Old Town section of the city. The cornice was eight floors up and in danger of falling on those who passed below.

Victor got the job on the strength of his earlier work for the Browns. But this job was far more complicated: the problem now was how to do it. Setting up scaffolding around the entire building would be expensive. Pop Croswell came up with a solution — a structure cantilevered out over the building, held in place by heavy sandbags on the roof, so that the workers could remove the failing cornice. The job was completed, but wound up costing more than the estimate. (Vic was terrified of heights, and had not gone up to the roof to take a close look at the situation to determine what the repairs would entail.) In the end, Baltimore Contractors lost about $1,200 on the job. That was a lot of money in those days, and word spread in local business circles.

Victor got a call to come to the railroad president's office.

"I understand you lost money on the job," Charles Brown said. "I want you to give me the figures on your cost overruns. We'll take care of them and give you a little something more for the job."

Victor thought for a moment about the unusual offer. He was a still a struggling young businessman, but Baltimore was a small town. He did not want to be bailed out. "Thank you Mr. Brown," he said. "I appreciate your offer. But I pay for my own mistakes."

Years later, Victor recalled this moment as the turning point of his business career. In fact, he called the Fidelity Warehouse the most profitable job he ever did. Just as word of his loss on the job got around town, so did his refusal to accept payment for more than he had bid. Baltimore Contractors not only could manage a big job well, they also stood behind their bids.

The phones started ringing.

IV. THE WOMAN BEHIND THE MAN

"The wife of an executive would be a better wife had she been a secretary first. As a secretary, you learn to adjust to the boss's moods. Many marriages would be happier if the wife would do that."

Anne Bogan

A picture of Margaret Frenkil taken in the middle-1950s shows a woman looking over her shoulder. She smiles with a contentment that reveals her positive, decidedly non-neurotic nature. It is a knowing smile, one that reflects her optimistic outlook on life. There is not a trace of doubt. It is the smile of serenity, kindness and confidence. Those who knew her well say there wasn't a hard edge to her personality. Everything about her was gentle, graceful, comforting.

She was, in many ways, the opposite of Victor. Whereas he was aggressive, she was softly persuasive. He was hyperactive, she was restrained. He was impatient, she was happy to take her time. He was devoted entirely to his business, and she to the family (with him very much at the center of it). He liked the company of important businessmen and politicians, while she liked the company of her children and close friends.

The marriage was a classic case of "opposites attract".

43

Victor and Margaret, despite their religious differences, made an excellent match. During their eight-year courtship, they got to know each other's personalities in depth. Margaret realized how Victor's offbeat mind worked, how he relished a challenge and let nothing stand in his way. She accepted his disregard for punctuality and his disdain for certain conventions. He never cared about his clothing, so she kept him in shirts, ties and suits. He misplaced or lost his hat so many times she had his name and address sewn inside it. She never objected to his one-AM telephoning and had a quick supper ready whenever he arrived hungry, often with three or four business associates in tow. While other couples were enjoying a quiet weekend breakfast, she was preparing a Saturday or

Margaret with first child, daughter, Janet, around 1933.

Sunday morning meal, frequently with Vic's associates present.

He admired her patience and her ability to stay with a project until it was completed. He also liked the joy she found in life's most simple tasks. Whether buying a new summer blanket or getting out the year's Christmas cards, Margaret was steady and cheerful. She did not criticize

Margaret's four children in the early 1940s: Janet, Victor Jr. (Bruz), Leonard and Vida (BeBe).

others and avoided gossip. She never complained and, if worried, she tended to keep it to herself.

From the very first, she assumed the role of a woman who was essentially giving — with her family, friends and many organizations in the city. Without her gentle powers of adjustment, remarkable tolerance and unusual ability to accommodate people, it is easy to believe that the marriage would not have lasted.

By all accounts the marriage of Victor and Margaret was a match as unusual as it was successful. In spite of (and perhaps because of) Vic's long hours away from home, they enjoyed each other's company. After fifty years of marriage, Margaret was still writing four words in her diary, a simple statement that meant so much to her, "Vic home for dinner" (this was undoubtedly noted since it was not an event that she could take for granted). And yet, she was able to avoid being annoyed when he worked late, showed up at strange hours or upset her day's plans. Her ability to give, understand, accept and even love the man for the kind of person he was swept aside the issues that might well have doomed the relationship. She simply loved being married to Victor Frenkil. And he, in his own way, reciprocated.

No doubt the loss of her father and two sisters in the 1918 Spanish influenza epidemic influenced Margaret's philosophy of life. Her mother had been widowed at the age of 30 and had no skills, so she scrubbed floors to help support her family. Then, as a young woman of 15, Margaret had to go to work to help the family, which she did without questioning. She attended a business school, where she learned to type and take shorthand, skills she would use all her life. If nothing else, this experience while still so young taught her resilience, an ability to bend, adjust and correct on the spot. Just as Victor could observe a situation and assess its strengths and weaknesses, Margaret forged her own judgments, set her own agenda. And, in a marriage of nearly seventy years, she set her priorities on others: her husband, sons and daughters, their children and a circle of relatives and friends.

Sometime in 1932 Margaret bought a pocket-sized diary. In it she wrote bits of philosophy and poetry that carried special meaning for her. The first entry, written in brown ink and dated 2 November 1932, is a poem from *McCall's Magazine*, "Reverie", by Raymond F. Broad. It captures her dreams, revealing a woman for whom marriage, family and the home were of prime importance. Her notes quote parts of it: "This is my dream, — cottage on a hill, set where the sun can flood it through with light, bowed with wide windows, smiling on the night…an inglenook for winter's evening dreams…you'd come, help me plan it, room by room…."

Over the years Margaret jotted more in her diary. She would not have taken the time and trouble to preserve these thoughts were they not important to her. The book is also well thumbed and its binding split, indications that she referred to its pages frequently.

"I do not know what your destiny will be, but this I do know — you will always have happiness if you seek and find how to serve." (Dr. Albert Schweitzer)

In her own handwriting, she wrote, "Go oft to the home of thy friend, for weeds choke up the unused path".

Another clipping, attributed to *Forbes Magazine*, says "Friendship implies loyalty, esteem, cordiality, sympathy, affection, readiness to aid, to help, to stick, to fight for, if need be. Radiate friendship and it will return sevenfold".

In 1963, she found a quotation from St. Francis de Sales: "Do not wish to be anything but what you are, and try to be that perfectly".

The harsh economics of the early days dictated that Margaret work alongside Victor in his first five or six years at Baltimore Contractors, the business he established at the time of their marriage. She certainly knew office routine. She had worked five years for the company that did the payroll for Victor's father's business, and no doubt had the chance to observe the Frenkil way of doing things. She was a meticulous worker. Her handwriting was clear and firm, and she could be frugal. She kept some of the young firm's first business records in one of Victor's discarded college binders.

When Margaret and Victor were first married, they rented a room from a Jewish widow. "She had several children and she had this one big room to rent out," Margaret recalled in the 1970s. "She gave us our bed and breakfast, which was always brown bread and sardines on Sundays. Today that is why Victor and I still have a Sunday morning tradition of brown bread and sardines. We were happy even though our life was very simple."

Their weekend morning meals became a tradition, often shared with friends and family members. Margaret made a salad of chopped lettuce and tomatoes, mixed with sardines and a special dressing, all prepared the way her first landlady had done in the early 1930s. It was the one time in the week when Victor was not on the move. It was a time that Margaret much enjoyed.

The young Frenkils were also practical. Margaret continued at her job at the John C. Knipp Company on Baltimore's Charles Street. Baltimore Contractors was a few blocks west on Park Avenue. At the end of the day, Margaret went to Victor's office and tallied the receipts of his business, wrote down the expenses and recorded the job orders.

There was never any doubt that they wanted a family. Margaret worked at the Knipp Company until she was four months pregnant, then devoted herself to her new role as mother. At the same time, she was never far away from Baltimore Contractors' accounts. After their first two children (Janet, then Vida) were born, Margaret employed live-in help to care for the two little girls so that she could return to her duties at the company.

She left the office each afternoon a little ahead of Victor, so that she could spend time with her daughters, prepare the evening meal, and have dinner and the house ready for Victor's return.

During the early 1930s, Margaret took an active role in the

A Baltimore Contractors party held at the Frenkils' Owings Mills estate, Wilton, which Victor used for annual summer picnics. Children were always welcome, and were generally found in the large swimming pool.

Business and Professional Women's Council, where she worked on getting legislation passed that would permit women to serve on juries. She was far ahead of her peers.

By about the time the Frenkils' two sons arrived — Victor Jr. in 1936 and Leonard in 1938, the business was well on its way to a solid footing. After six or seven years of keeping the books, Margaret gradually stepped aside. The business had in fact grown too large for her. Victor's work was taking him all over the city and state. And, in his absences, Margaret settled in as a full-time mother.

About ten years into the marriage, Victor started looking for a farm for a business friend of his and, in the process, found and recommended the magnificent old Gutman estate in Owings Mills. It would make a fabulous place to entertain with its 38 acres, manicured gardens, large and comfortable home, outbuildings and a long, curving (and impressive) driveway with two large pillars at the entrance. But his friend chose to buy elsewhere. So Victor decided to buy the estate, called "Wilton".

Baltimore Contractors had been building a swimming pool a short distance from Wilton, so Victor, in his opportunistic way, took full advantage of the situation. He finished the job and moved the forms and equipment to his new estate, where he built a large pool for business entertaining as well as for the family. He also built a tennis court and, in his inventive way, altered the basic design. He liked to ice skate, so he sunk the tennis court six inches into the ground, set up a special drainage system and flooded it in winter.

Wilton demonstrated how well his business was doing, and gave him the room to hold the huge parties he liked to throw, complete with fortune tellers, magicians, pony and choo-choo train rides for the children, sumptuous meals and, of course, swimming and tennis for those so disposed. It also gave Margaret and the four children a larger, more comfortable home in a nicer and quieter location.

Margaret adjusted easily to this new phase of her life. Several times a year she would be hostess for the large company parties Victor liked

Victor and Margaret at one of the many fundraisers they attended, this one in 1959.

to throw for several hundred guests from the transportation, business, legal and political communities that he cultivated. Margaret managed everything: placement of umbrellas, tables and chairs, planning the menu, overseeing the cooking and serving staff, all the while keeping an eye on her four children. Throughout her life Margaret remained faithful to her simple

A rare occasion when Vic was willing to leave the business behind to be with Margaret — with no telephone.

ways. She usually set aside one day a week to visit Baltimore's downtown department stores, where she spent most of her time gathering practical gifts for her children and, later, grandchildren. (If her diaries give a clear picture, she spent more time having her shoes fitted with corrective inserts to assist in comfortable walking than she did in the actual purchase of the footwear.)

Ever the family matriarch, she maintained strong friendships with her in-laws. She remained close to her mother and sister Elizabeth, her sisters-in-law Sophie, Celia, Sadie, Ida and Rose, and her brothers George and Joe, who had taken Roman Catholic religious orders and become a Marianist brother. She stayed in constant contact with her circle of loved ones, either by phone or by visiting them. To those laid up in a hospital or nursing home, she was a frequent visitor.

Margaret clearly enjoyed doing things for others. For most

Margaret's favorite and long-standing "Sewing Circle". From left: Lillian Zonmiller, Margaret, Lillian Aaron, Kathleen Ward, Monica McGeady.

of her adult life she was a weekly volunteer at one of her favorite charities, Children's Hospital, where she arranged small gifts for bedridden children who had to endure lengthy stays. Margaret also sat on the board of the Maryland Chapter of the Cystic Fibrosis Foundation, and devoted many hours to planning fundraising functions. She was also a generous donor.

In 1953, about the time Vic was working on the Cancer Society's annual campaign, Margaret became the co-chair of Jewish Appeal for Associated Jewish Charities. Newspaper stories credit her with setting up the social structure through which thousands of families and individuals received a personal visit. She helped organize a massive weekend drive, headquartered at the Fifth Regiment Armory, in which all her captains moved throughout the city, rang doorbells and solicited financial pledges. She continued her work for the Associated Jewish Charities for many years. She also belonged to The Children's Guild, the St. Elizabeth Guild, the Women's Civic League, the American Jewish Committee, and the Women's

Grandmother for the first time: A thrilled Margaret holds Jeff Kreiger, her first of 14 grandchildren, in the living room at Wilton in 1959.

Margaret at her happiest: with the family (1950). Back, left to right are Janet, Margaret, Victor, Bebe. Front, left to right, Leonard and Victor Jr.

A happy Grandmother Margaret surrounded by nine of her many grandchildren. Photo taken around 1962.

Board of the Johns Hopkins Hospital, among many others.

Margaret's photograph appeared in Baltimore newspapers many times over the years. She was treasurer of the Baltimore Symphony Orchestra's Women's Association in the mid-1950s. She was, with her experience, excellent with money and kept the books meticulously. She also had the same job with the Baltimore Opera Guild, where she remained an officer (and subscriber) for decades.

Ever a careful record keeper, Margaret maintained a ledger of all her expenses, household and otherwise. What is striking about its details are the many gifts she gave and contributions she made.

She also became a friend to the wives of several of Victor's business associates, especially Monica McGeady, Lillian Aaron, Kathleen Ward and Lillian Zonmiller. They called themselves the "Sewing Circle" and met for lunches and cocktails regularly for many years.

"I remember coming home from school and seeing my mother and Margaret dressed in white gloves and veiled hats," said F. X. McGeady. "None of the ladies drove cars and my brothers or I would pick up Margaret or drop her off at the Marylander."

When Victor didn't have the time to travel, Margaret and some of these women would take a trip on their own. On one occasion, Margaret and Monica McGeady took a trip that went around the world, with stops in Asia and India. The two friends had a marvelous experience (so marvelous, in fact, that they had to wire home for additional funds).

After Margaret's children had left home, these women provided a social basis for weekly lunches and matinee trips to Baltimore's theaters. Margaret loved music, both opera and symphonies, and had her own seats in the Lyric's center balcony. And while she could not get Victor to accompany her to the opera often, she succeeded on occasion — sometimes resulting in their inviting the entire cast back to Wilton for refreshments afterwards. If Victor could not go, she attended with family members or friends. And yet, on these evenings, Victor was never far away. In her handwriting, among her daily calendar entries, she would write, "Met up with Vic late, had a snack and went home".

That was what mattered to Margaret — closing the family circle at the end of the day, no matter how late.

While Margaret could be (and often was) firm with her husband, it was her devotion that made it possible for Victor to be as successful as he was. She handled everything outside of Baltimore Contractors, so he could concentrate entirely on what he did best — and loved to do most — his business.

In his later years, when Vic turned to writing songs as a pastime, he wrote one entitled, "My Margaret". These are the lyrics he composed on 20 August 1994:

My Margaret, my Margaret, is gentle and sweet,
She's the loveliest lady you'll ever want to meet.
From the day of her birth,
She's been an angel on earth.
She's brought romance to my life,
How lucky I've been to have her for my wife.
I have lived a life divine,
Because my Margaret has always been mine.
Her poetic voice
Rings out with rejoice.
My Margaret, my Margaret, is gentle and sweet,
She's the loveliest lady you'll ever want to meet!

V. Life In
The Fast Lane

"Work is love made visible. And if you cannot work with love but only with distaste, it is better that you should leave your work and sit at the gate of the temple and take alms of those who work with joy."

Khalil Gibran

Victor Frenkil was a man in a hurry, having chosen to live life in high gear. He was at his best when he was on the way to an appointment, usually late, with a phone call or two waiting, while he was still on the car phone. He existed on very little sleep, although he would often close his eyes for a ten-minute nap, then wake up refreshed with energy that could weary those around him.

Victor's lifestyle was maddening to those not accustomed to his perpetual motion, the probing mental activity and the insatiable curiosity that led to endless requests.

Victor was an early riser, and Margaret got up with him so the two of them could have breakfast together, since she rarely knew whether he would be home for dinner (and rarely did he at that early hour). He moved briskly, always kissing Margaret goodbye before leaving for work sometime around 7:00 in the morning. He was generally dressed in a light suit, and he carried a felt hat.

Wasting time was something he did not understand. For most of his life, he did not drive (which was probably a blessing for other drivers because, when he did take the wheel, he ignored most of the rules of the road to get where he wanted to go). He found he could make better use of the time if he sat in the back, with a chauffeur driving, and concentrated on the plans for the day. Nearly 40 years before cell phones were commonplace, Victor had one of the earliest radio-powered models installed in his car. George McManus, his friend and attorney, recalled getting early calls from him, some before dawn.

"If he was up, the world was up," said his son, Victor Jr., referring to his father's desire to be surrounded by activity at every waking moment.

Victor's workday started well before he arrived at the office. Jerry Jarosinski, one of his vice-presidents, often picked him up at his front door. He would occasionally ask to detour to one of his own construction projects — or to another site, maybe that of a competitor, just to satisfy his fervent curiosity. Then he would take the first of his many catnaps on the way to the office.

If a car and driver, engine running and ready to take him to the office, were not waiting, he would cross the street to hail a cab or a passing motorist he may have vaguely known. Victor Frenkil seemed to be acquainted with half of Baltimore. If he did not know someone, he would introduce himself and chatter away as if they were old friends. In doing so, Victor demonstrated an infectious, ingratiating side of his personality. He could greet, and talk to anyone he met, no matter who the person was. It was a trait that served him well.

By one means or another, he arrived at his office every day about 7:15. He was frequently the first.

Always arriving ten or fifteen minutes later (tardiness that Victor chose to overlook, given her remarkable talents) was Virginia Lambrow, his corporate secretary, deputy and vice-president for more than 40 years. Virginia was much more than a secretary. She was a gal Friday, personal assistant, time manager, appointment maker, information gatherer, chief scheduler, social consultant, prime organizer. Remarkably intelligent, unusually perceptive and totally discreet, she wrought order out of the chaos that seemed to follow Victor wherever he went.

Tall and imperious, her very bearing commanded respect. She was Greek, and intensely proud of her Greek background, which led to deep involvement within the Greek community in Baltimore. She never married, dedicating her life to Victor

and Baltimore Contractors, caring for her mother, and helping other Greeks. There was no one who dared question her authority. And there are some who say that

Virginia Lambrow with her mother at a BCI function.

she was in large part responsible for the success that Victor achieved.

"Miss Virginia" (women at Baltimore Contractors were called "Miss") read the morning paper for him during her first years with BCI and typed summaries of reports that would be of interest. Articles of political interest came first. And while

Victor enjoyed seeing his own name in print, he was more interested in looking for clues about potential contracting jobs. He would have a secretary boil down certain articles and circulate them among his executives. If a story caught his interest, he would often phone the reporter and proceed to interview him just as casually as he had earlier flagged down the driver who didn't know he was going Victor's way until that morning.

For nearly 60 years Victor's office was at 711 South Central Avenue, a street number Victor had assigned to the site for its easy memorability. Baltimore Contractors was housed in a two-story 1930s building of dark brown, rustic-style bricks.

The construction industry traditionally gets off to an early start. And when Victor stepped through the office door, the telephone operators, secretaries, engineers and clerks who happened to be there knew that they would be commanded into action almost immediately.

On most mornings, the first thing he did was to get on the telephone. He tortured the phone lines, and Broadway 6-2800 became one of the most-used numbers in the city. Colleagues at Baltimore Contractors said one of the hardest-working employees was the telephone operator, who, in addition to putting through dozens of calls per hour on a manual, spaghetti-plug switchboard, also had to

Victor chats up a secretary and solidifies a useful link.

keep track of the boss' movements. Further, she had to be able to track down anyone he wanted on a moment's notice. (One employee recalled being sent to the reference room of the city library for some information on a project done some 40 years prior, only to have the librarian hand him a phone on his arrival and say "Mr. Frenkil wants to talk with you".)

"At times we practically had to hide the phone from him," Virginia Lambrow said. "And because of the volume of calls, we definitely had to keep some calls away from him."

Over the years Victor perfected a method for charming people. He could extract favors from casual friendships and acquaintances. It was not by chance that he got to know the drivers, secretaries and aides of governors, mayors and other elected officials. He was friendly to maids and servants as well. He flattered them, occasionally giving them tickets to oyster feasts and bull roasts. He also got their private telephone numbers and home addresses.

Victor knew that access was power. If he was a friend of these people, he could count on their help in reaching a higher-up whom he would one day want to see. He believed that any door could be opened to him; no one, no matter his or her station or power level, was unreachable or untouchable. Further, he enjoyed these social and business conquests.

"He could find anybody, no matter where they were," recalled Jerry Jarosinski.

On one occasion, a BCI executive, Charles Callanan, was driving to New England on vacation. Victor wanted to speak to him. Never mind that he had left no phone numbers. He called one of his contacts, a high official of the Maryland State police, who, in turn, called his counterpart in Massachusetts. A police radio message went out to watch for a certain car with Maryland license plates. Not much later, a state police officer

Lyndon B. Johnson welcomes Victor to the Rose Garden at the White House.

pulled Mr. Callanan over and gave him the message to call Mr. Frenkil.

The lengths he went to reach people knew no bounds. He had Johns Hopkins heart surgeon, Dr. Levi Watkins, summoned from the operating room. He interrupted one of his attorneys, J. Martin Jones, on his honeymoon in Nantucket.

One day in the 1960s, he called Jerry Jarosinski into his office and told him they were going to drive to South Baltimore. Nothing more was said. Victor didn't seem to have a specific destination in mind, but when he saw a group of police cars, he told Jerry to drive to where they were. An officer walked up to the car. Victor lowered the window, gave his name and he was immediately waved through. Within a few minutes a helicopter landed and President Lyndon B. Johnson emerged. The President walked through the crowd and saluted in his Texas drawl, "Hi, Vic".

On another trip, Victor traveled with USF&G executive

Charles Foelber to Salisbury for the funeral of Governor Millard Tawes, an old-school Democrat with whom Victor had close personal ties. As usual, they were late and the parking lot at the church was filled. State troopers were posted at the front of the Salisbury Methodist church, where the services were being held. Victor told Charles to ignore all the "no parking" signs and pull up in front of the church, alongside the hearse. Charles momentarily resisted, then did as Victor requested. A state trooper came up to wave them away, at which point Victor rolled down the window. "Hi, Mr. Frenkil," the trooper said, adding that it was perfectly fine to park the car there.

His ability to search out and meet people was legendary. "I don't think he ever felt there was anybody beyond his grasp," said Victor Jr. "There was no one he couldn't reach. There was nothing he couldn't do. He loved the challenge of it. It was far more important to him than making money."

Victor had a distinct pattern of behavior in the office. He was a nonstop micro-manager. "He always had a better way of doing it, no matter what it was," said his son. He dictated hundreds of memos to his staff. Each of these directives was typed on a slip of easily noticed pink paper. Their frequency drove his people crazy. No matter how quickly they tried to comply with his suggestions, suddenly another pink missive would arrive.

"He could be a very demanding person," Jerry Jarosinski recalled. "But if, over time, he found out that you knew what you were talking about, he sometimes left you alone."

This comment notwithstanding, Victor was not a genuine delegator, especially when it came to important decisions. He was the classic entrepreneur used to doing everything himself, incapable of letting go as the world he built grew and increased in complexity (one of the reasons he worked such long hours).

President George H. W. Bush and the first lady chat with Victor. Comfortable playing both sides, Vic was friend to Republican and Democrat alike.

Always a tough competitor, Vic wins the sack race at the annual BCI picnic (this one on 26 July 1947). In spite of the heat, Vic races wearing a necktie.

In spite of having hired some highly professional and talented people, his incessant meddling reminded all that no decision of any import was to be taken in his absence.

Victor's office was at the top of a long staircase that led to the second floor. It was paneled in dark wood (salvaged from an old Silber's Bakery) and was cluttered comfortably with memorabilia. On the walls were hung pictures of Victor with the rich, famous and powerful, including presidents Lyndon Johnson and George Bush. There was also a picture of a rail-road bridge over Aquia Creek in Virginia, a place where Victor once nearly defaulted on a construction project. He did not, but only through some major Frenkilesque gymnastics. He kept the picture on display as a daily reminder of how easily a job could go wrong.

Vic with South Africa's Bishop Desmond Tutu and Maryland Comptroller Louis Goldstein.

He also displayed a sampler his mother had made. Its embroidered letters said, "Plan your work. Work your plan". He lived by this rule.

His door was always closed and, to reach him, one first had to get past the formidable Virginia Lambrow. Victor's two favorite business tools were the telephone and a buzzer system. In addition to the main switchboard, Victor kept a second, private number, known only to his closest friends and certain family members. It was over this private line that millions and millions of dollars of business was conducted.

He had a buzzer code. One long sound summoned Virginia Lambrow. Two short buzzes brought his secretary. One short buzz was a signal that he was ready to receive those who were waiting outside. There was also a panic buzz, a signal for all hands to render immediate assistance. He blasted the panic buzzer when he was on the phone with a client and needed help with numbers or a report to be passed hurriedly under his eyes, so he could impress his caller with an instant recall of a project.

An important part of Victor Frenkil's life was a steady stream of people with whom he interacted, and his day was not complete without having many visitors in his office. They were salesmen, city council members, important politicians, international dignitaries. He counted it a good day when he entertained or discussed some idea he was hatching with a mayor, county executive or business tycoon.

He felt there was never enough time to do all he wanted to, and this was reflected in a few rules he enforced in the office. He did not permit employees to linger in the corridors. As he moved about, he would often say, "Get out of the halls and get back to work". He also did not approve of his workers lingering over the coffee pot. One cup of coffee per morning was allowed. He had a small sign printed that was placed in all the offices as a reminder of his philosophy that read "NOW!"

He provided a free hot lunch to his entire office staff, which generally ran between 30 and 40 persons. There was a company dining room (also decorated with pictures of job sites and important persons, especially U.S. presidents) and a cook. There was a head table for the executives, where he presided when he was not out of the office.

He left and returned to 711 South Central Avenue five or

six times a day, and was almost always late for his next appointment.

Victor frequently called meetings. They tended to be protracted sessions with his department heads. He sat at the head of the table and, as the meeting wore on, often appeared to nod off as his lieutenants read their reports. (Victor was a fanatic about reports, and

Vic never tired of being seen with the famous and influential, this time with President Clinton.

would have them prepared in remarkable detail. He believed that, if you made someone report the details of what he was responsible for, that person was far more likely to do his job.) While he appeared to be asleep, he could nevertheless respond to what they said. Many thought the meetings were unnecessarily long. He never took notes, but always had others ready with a spiral-bound book for this purpose. He sat at the big table and folded his dollar bills into initials and designs, hour after hour, day after day (a habit he pursued for many years). Doing two things at the same time was commonplace for him.

Business colleagues, the men he had hired, said he rarely heeded their advice. "I would attend the executive meetings," said Edward Hanrahan, his former director of publicity and marketing. "But in time, I grew rather bored. He never really took me into his confidence."

In spite of the time he spent with the influential people

who could help him achieve his goals, Victor rarely carried money. When there was a bill to be paid, such as a quick lunch outside the office, he would ask one of his employees to pay it. Then he would tell him to submit an expense account and have it reimbursed by the comptroller.

Several times a day Victor and his project managers left the office to inspect jobs. Victor had a rule for this, too. If you took one route to get there, you returned by a different one, no matter how complicated. This circumnavigation appealed to his penchant for odd practices. If they got lost, he had his driver stop the car so he could get out and ask directions from the first person he met.

Another manifestation of the pace at which he lived was his total disregard for one-way streets and traffic signals. He viewed them as impediments to the speedy completion of whatever he was doing. If he had a destination, all he wanted to do was to get there. Traffic signs meant nothing, even when he was accompanied by bankers and bonding-company people who often went along on a job. It was Victor's way of doing business: "NOW!"

Victor's day did not end when the sun went down. He was only shifting into the second phase. Margaret knew his hours were his own. He might be home for dinner and he might not, a decision generally made at the last minute depending on whether he thought he could further his business by dining with a prospect.

He enjoyed entertaining and often held business dinners nearby in Baltimore's Little Italy, especially at Maria's at 500 Albemarle Street, a restaurant he had remodeled years before. He liked to have potential customers at the table, and often added several politicians to demonstrate his influence and help win the job. Friends said he ate everything and liked his foods swimming in butter. He disliked dry dishes and would send them back to have more sauce or gravy added. He had a weakness for Lobster Fra Diablo and was fond of fruit. He rarely drank alcohol, although sometimes he would have half a glass of beer with steamed crabs or a half-strength Bloody Mary. At Maria's, he table-hopped when he spotted a local — and occasional a national — celebrity.

One of his day's great joys was circulating at a bull roast, crab feast or business dinner party, where he could move from table to table and be Baltimore's social butterfly. He would normally buy two tables at fund-raising dinners to be able to have 20 or more guests in his party. He liked having his employees' spouses along. And when at a large function, he wanted them to fan out among the other guests and make themselves known, helping raise the visibility of Baltimore Contractors. He did not let his people talk among themselves, insisting on the roving ambassadorial role. He also liked to mix in other guests, often drawn from his political and business lists, at these functions. It was his way of making sure that Baltimore Contractors was well known in the community. Recognition, he felt, translated into business.

Each Preakness Day he would charter a bus and escort a large party to Pimlico Race Course. He never bet because he knew the odds were against him, a risk he would not take (although he did occasionally shoot craps). He knew the annual sporting event would be filled with all sorts of potential business contacts — and worked the club house for hours, hobnobbing with the lawyers, bankers, advertising executives, society people, reporters and politicians that defined his sphere of power.

"He was always on the go, a perpetual motion machine that day," recalled his friend, Charles Foelber. "The rest of us came home exhausted. He was probably on the phone making another five or six calls."

At the very end of the day, ready to dismiss his engineers from one of these banquets, he would shake their hands and say, "Go home, get a good night's rest. And pick me up at 7 tomorrow morning".

He would go home and greet Margaret affectionately, then pick up the phone to call the man who had just driven him home minutes earlier.

"I'd just have dropped him and my wife would be saying, 'It's Victor Frenkil calling you,'" Jerry Jarosinski said. "He had another thought in his mind and he couldn't wait until morning."

Then, as a reminder that he was always ready to help, he would add, "Call me if there's anything I can do for you".

The odd thing was that he meant it.

VI. THE
UNSPENDABLE DOLLAR

*"Today he has the perhaps unparalleled ability to make
words up to five letters long with one dollar bill."*

The Baltimore Sun, 1964

Turning dollar bills into highly personalized keepsakes may have been Victor Frenkil's most successful calling card, a hobby that made him a "man of letters". The man who built a good-sized chunk of the Chesapeake Bay Bridge, renovated and owned the city's most venerable hotel and hobnobbed with presidents, had a unique talent: He could fold dollar bills intricately (and unceasingly), never mutilating them, never cutting them. For a man who hardly ever wrote and whose handwriting was illegible, his signature became the dollar bill. He was literally the man who signed his name with folded money.

A newspaper interviewer reported that, during the 1968 Democratic National Convention in Chicago, while Vietnam War protesters were exchanging blows with police outdoors and politicians were battling for power indoors, Mr. Frenkil sat quietly with his colleagues in the Maryland delegation, working his fingers "almost unconsciously and turning out one

Vic at his favorite hobby: creating origami out of one-dollar bills.

monetary monogram after another".

"It's very relaxing and distracting. I call it creative ingenuity. It keeps me from going to sleep during meetings," he told *The Sun's* Robert Erlandson in 1996. During this interview, a few years before his death, he disclosed some of his paper-folding techniques. "You have to visualize the whole thing in advance. You have to see it finished; you can't just think of one letter at a time." This could indeed have been a reference to the way he lived his life. His actions were rarely isolated. Victor Frenkil had a way of weaving people, talent, opportunity and business into one integrated piece of work.

Victor's ability to take a bill and fold it into the initials of its recipient was a stunning personal public relations gift, one that continues to outlive its author. His bill-folding ability earned him 50 years of newspaper photographs, feature stories and good "buzz" on the street. It was the kind of publicity that money couldn't buy (although in its own curious way, it did just that).

Victor liked inviting friends and business associates to dine with him, but these events were quickly forgotten. The key chains, nail clippers, pens and memo pads he passed out bearing the name of Baltimore Contractors may have made an impression, but eventually were tossed out. Nobody, however, threw away his initials neatly folded from a single dollar bill. Victor was able to turn cash into keepsakes.

"I get letters from people all over the country asking me to make initials for them," Victor said in 1996.

At that time he estimated that he had folded "a minimum of $15,000" over the years. It was probably a low estimate. Had he folded fifty one-dollar bills a month for the 57 years his nimble fingers carried out his craft, he would have spent nearly $35,000 on this hobby.

Virginia Lambrow, Victor's executive secretary, said, "I've watched him do this for a long time. He formed a template in his mind and then made the bill fit it".

It could take him half an hour or all day to work out the plan and execute it, depending on the letters. "The letter D is the most difficult to use because of its shape," he said in the 1996 *Sun* interview.

He started out folding two initials. Then, challenged as always, he moved to three initials and, comfortable with that, went on to four and occasionally five and even six. "I have done four initials, but it's a rarity that I can do more than that," he said. Then he pointed to examples of "Jimmy, Johnny, Billy and Merry" to show there were exceptions.

"Each one is a different challenge because the combination of initials is infinite. I have to plan it when I start, down to an eighth of an inch because of the size of a dollar bill and the different sizes of letters," said Victor, who had been born left-handed, although his father forced him to use his right hand, which led to his ambidexterity.

In his office was a triptych frame of items he had made in origami style using dollar bills, including flying and standing birds, pinwheels, a peacock, trousers and a sofa. There were bow ties, picture frames, rings and other pieces too, all made from new, crisp, one-dollar bills. On occasion he'd made a duck with wings that flapped when its tail was pulled.

"I've never studied origami," he said. "I've just seen pictures of these things and then worked them out for myself. U.S. currency is printed on the toughest paper ever made," and was perfect for his craft, he said.

The 1996 article said Victor did not suffer from arthritis or rheumatism. (Throughout his long life he was rarely sick, although he was happy to allow downtime for those who were.) Until the end, his long fingers retained the strength and dexterity required to fold money with the creativity and precision he brought to the task.

"He begins by pleating a bill lengthwise in eighth-inch-wide folds until it becomes a long, narrow strip. He then unfolds it and applies his magic. His fingers knead the paper, folding and shaping, until, with a flourish, he presents the monogram," *The Sun* noted.

None of the many articles written in Baltimore about him made mention that, as early as 1958, he had been named an honorary member of the Origami Center, founded by paper-folding pioneers Lillian Oppenheimer and Akira Yoshizawa. Leaders in the art of paper folding, they were fascinated by his wing-flapping duck folded from a dollar bill and visited him in Baltimore at a breakfast meeting with Victor's friend Jimmy Swartz.

"The essence of Victor Frenkil's technique was that

Nancy Reagan and Frank Sinatra receive dollar-bill initials from Victor in November of 1984.

he pleated the dollar bill into narrow pleats longitudinally and then used reverse folding to turn the corners of the letters and numbers. There have been other systems of folding the alphabet from money and similar techniques have been applied to the Hebrew alphabet, but so far as I know, Victor Frenkil's was the first system and was entirely his own inspiration," said David Lister, an origami historian from Grimsby, England.

Victor said his most difficult challenge came in 1948, when a Californian wrote to ask whether he could fold a bill into a five-pointed star. Each angle had to be 72 degrees, and he experimented for months before working out the solution by geometry. It required 52 foldings, twice the usual number for a monogram.

He also recorded some of his techniques in a 1968 book, *Folding Money, Vol. 2.*

His interviewer asked if his sons and daughters had learned his hobby. "I can teach them the technique, but they have to figure out each one, and most people don't have the time or the

Vic gives "R M NIXON" in folded dollar bills to the Vice-President.

patience to do it," Victor said. This proved not to be accurate. His son, Victor, is an excellent paper folder, who very much duplicates his father's efforts and often sits in business meetings doing just the same thing. He, too, combats boredom by folding money.

Occasionally, Victor invited another paper-folding enthusiast to duplicate his work by sending two monograms, one to keep and the other to unfold to try to see how it was done. Victor said no one had met his challenge and that he expected to remain champion as long as his fingers would let him.

Victor said a returning World War II G.I. had taught him the technique of how to fold a bow tie from a dollar as well as how to fold a bill so that it showed George Washington in the center of a small frame. The soldier had mastered the trick of their construction during long, boring days overseas. Victor said he spent two days attempting to duplicate them. When he realized he was unable to, he brought the fellow back and asked for another demonstration. It still took three weeks of practice before he had command of these two works of art.

Victor's folded bills were unique, presents that reflected the personality of their maker. For all Victor's quirks, it was the folded money that most captured his lifestyle, his ability to twist things around to his liking, to size up a situation at a moment's notice, to throw an adversary off his guard and gain entry into his world.

His folded money opened doors for him, led to recognition and, in a curious way, often cemented business friendships. Through his secretary, Virginia Lambrow, he mailed thousands of these dollar bills. She kept meticulous records and duplicate copies of the requests for initials and other objects made from paper money. No doubt the cost of the office overhead and behind-the-scenes correspondence far outweighed the actual dollar mailed.

Victor's small gifts were perceived to have significant value by those who received them. They conveyed the notion of his generosity and thoughtfulness. They were intensely personal, not just because the initials were those of the recipient, but also because he had taken the time to create them. They often caught people off guard. After all, you don't get a personalized "moneygram" every day.

His hobby spoke much about him. Victor was a complicated individual who was not guided by conventions. He was a generous, ambitious man, but one who felt the necessity to be in constant control. He was a man who slept little and worked all his waking hours. He folded his money during car rides and during meetings. He folded his money while he spoke on the phone. He folded his money during important business conversations. Some thought it odd that, even during the most trouble-filled chapters of his life, he often sat, said little and folded money. In a sense, the bills were his version of worry beads. While his successes were not always well understood, or his charity recognized by the public, his folding of dollar bills carried with it recognition, attention and a celebrity status.

The paper-folding also fit Victor's penchant for being dif-

"Merry Xmas and Happy New Year Lyndon B Johnson" in dollars, presented to President Johnson by Vic. All words except "Lyndon" and "Johnson" are folded from single bills.

ferent. He was a man who could never master driving a car well. Yet he rode a unicycle and frequently demonstrated his prowess to his children by riding a bicycle while sitting on the handlebars — backward. He also took up the pogo stick and bounced around skillfully when he felt like it.

He used his dollar bills as an entry vehicle. He would have his secretary call someone whose who attention he sought to ask them their middle initial. A few days later, a wallet-size plastic carrying case would arrive with the folded money inside. Its appeal was hard to resist. You might not know what to do with it, but you didn't throw it out. And you never forgot who had sent it.

How did it all begin? Politics, of course. Victor said he got the idea in 1940, during one of Wendell Willkie's presidential campaigns, when a Republican staff member devised a way of folding dollar bills in the letter W. Victor left no account of how many telephone calls he made, or letters he wrote, to the unnamed woman in Washington who knew the principles of

Margaret and Victor present a "HHH" to Senator Hubert H. Humphrey.

Luciano Pavarotti gets his initials from Vic at the Belvedere Hotel.

Maryland Governor William Donald Schaefer receives an unusual contribution:"You will win Don for Gov of USA" in single dollar bills.

what is called Origami, or the Japanese art of paper folding (a term he never used).

"I was immediately intrigued," Victor said in a 1964 *Baltimore Sun* interview about his hobby.

Victor took his folded dollar bills wherever he did (or wanted to do) business, and, on two occasions, took his money right to the Presidential Oval Office of the White House.

"Jack Kennedy sent a personal check for $10 to the Cancer Society," he said (Victor suggested the recipient make a donation rather than give a dollar back to him).

It was the initials that created the photo-opportunity sessions at the White House. He was photographed with then-Vice-President Richard M. Nixon. In this case, each letter in the Nixon name was a separate bill and the whole composition was framed so, when both men were photographed, the composition would show well.

By the time Lyndon B. Johnson sat in the Oval Office, Victor's folding abilities were well advanced. His 1964

Christmas-New Year's greeting to the president, framed like a sampler, was a riot of acute angles. He managed to form the word "Merry" out of one bill. Only the proper names "Lyndon" and "Johnson" required two bills, which were then affixed to each other with tape.

In the 1964 *Sun* interview, he said, "I can make a 'W', why can't I make all the other letters?" The he spent the next five years fiddling with dollars bills until he mastered the alphabet. "Today he has the perhaps unparalleled ability to make words up to five letters long with one dollar bill," the 1964 article reported.

By the 1960s he was using his folded money like a one-man public-relations campaign. His

Victor presents a single dollar folded into the initials "WJC" to President W. J. Clinton.

sets of initials, often packed in a plastic sleeve with the Baltimore Contractors, Inc., logo, name and address imprinted on it, were being set to politicians, bank officials, lawyers and anyone Victor wanted to meet or flatter. When the newspaper articles started broadcasting his ability to fold money, he generously complied with all requests.

His signature pieces were auctioned at charity fundraisers and church bazaars. In a city that relished curious folksy customs of many kinds, he achieved celebrity status. He was the man who could make your initials out of a dollar that you'd never spend.

He never accepted any money for his dollars, preferring a donation to a charity (the American Cancer Society was his favorite).

His son, Victor Jr., recalled that his father's form of charity became so well known that the Internal Revenue

Victor at his desk with one-dollar bills on the way to becoming unforgettable (and unspendable) gifts for special people.

Service surprisingly permitted a tax deduction for his hobby.

Along with the American Cancer Society, the Rotary Club benefited each year from Victor's skill. He earned $500 for the club at its annual oyster roast, selling initials and such items as tie clips, birds and rings made from folded bills.

At his peak of folding money, he kept about fifty new dollar bills in his desk, ready for the next opportunity to please someone in his unique way.

Of course, Victor's secretaries filled scrapbooks with the letters of thanks and acknowledgement his folded money brought. Film star Greer Garson, who received a GG, thanked Victor by calling the dollar a "handy dandy piece of mad money".

But the majority of his dollars went to people who merely asked for them. They went to individuals at the Chamber of Commerce and Lion's Club banquets. They also went to the drivers and personal staff of persons with whom he did business, because, to Victor, the folded dollars were as important a piece of business equipment as a blueprint, a backhoe or a concrete mixer.

He had many variations, too. He made roses with bills for the petals and offered them at charity events for $20 each.

"I usually only sell a few of those, to guys who want to impress their girl friends," he said, adding that they are the

One of Victor's more unusual creations: a duck whose wings flapped when its tail was pulled (folded from a single dollar bill).

same men who ask him to make initials out of $100 bills — also for their sweethearts.

It is curious that such a complicated and precise art was executed so brilliantly by a man who, in addition to his reading problems, could barely sign his name. His personal signature was a compressed, illegible jumble of scribbled ink.

His secretaries suffered when he composed a letter. He would dictate words and sentences. Once typed, he would have the text read back, then order more changes. This process might be repeated several times. There is one story of a letter being rewritten 27 times, about the same number of folds in one of his dollar-bill creations.

Victor delighted in the publicity that newspaper articles about his hobby generated. And he genuinely liked meeting people this way.

That is why today, some years after his death, many people, from the famous to the obscure, remember Victor Frenkil as the man who folded their initials from a dollar bill.

VII. Politician
Without Office

"Man is by nature a political animal."
Aristotle

Victor Frenkil thrived in the whirlwind of political life. For a man who never ran for or held elected office, he followed candidates and their programs the way diehard sports fans follow baseball. A 1977 *Baltimore Sun* article said it well: "Everybody knows Vic Frenkil. He's been around for years. You're in politics in Maryland — you know Vic Frenkil. He's everywhere".

Victor not only mixed his socializing with those in the construction business and those who held elective office: they *were* his social life. If a new school was going up, he knew its principal and those on the board of public works who let the contract. He befriended the important and those who supported them. Once he won them over, he could begin to exercise the persuasive power of his personality — at which he excelled.

His critics would say that Victor Frenkil staged big parties and picked up dinner checks because he wanted to cast a wide net of influence and win profitable governmental considerations. A profile on him in *The Sun* in 1977 put it this way:

"Frenkil, shrewd workaholic, prospers as omnipresent friend of power".

In fact, while in his late 80s, long after his days as a powerful contractor, Victor Frenkil was still throwing parties and picking up checks. The man simply loved orchestrating events populated by influential people. "He likes to identify himself with people in office," said his old friend and Wednesday-night dinner companion, Charles L. Benton. "Whether it benefits him or not, I don't know, but he likes to be seen with them."

Victor's world of politics, crab feasts, Preakness parties, oyster roasts and testimonial dinners began about the time he founded Baltimore Contractors in the 1930s. It may have started with his annual Christmas parties, at which he supplied plenty of food, cheer and good times. Who knows the first time he brought a friend home to Margaret's kitchen for a home-cooked meal (probably with little or no advance warning to his wife).

Perhaps these gatherings were an extension of the personality traits he displayed at Forest Park High School, where he was the center of attention at so many events, yet always slightly behind the scenes, making things work just so, then strolling into the principal's office without an appointment to work his magic and achieve his ends. His friends, simply stated, were the people who wrote him the checks for bridges and concrete work. They were also his building-material suppliers, bankers, and insurance agents. Also, just for good measure, he liked to have newspaper columnists, colleagues from the religious and charitable causes he served and more than a few hangers-on around to fill out a room. And when in the room, rarely taking a microphone or standing in the spotlight, he could talk and circulate from table to table, group to group. He was far more a private manipulator than a public figure. Brilliant behind the scenes, he avoided the stage, leaving it to those who wanted such public acclaim (he much preferred exerting his influence over those whose opinions mattered).

"He was a charmer," said George McManus, an attorney who handled his business affairs. "It was very hard not to like Victor Frenkil."

Even his critics would admit that he never forgot anyone. And should a friend die, he remembered his wife with flowers and cards for many years — an indication that it was more than influence and power that motivated him. Once a friend of Victor Frenkil, there was a bond of loyalty established that he never forgot.

The first decade of Victor's leadership at Baltimore Contractors was successful, but, as its president, he wanted larger jobs, the kind the city's largest general contractors routinely won. These golden prizes came from City Hall and the Annapolis State House and, in the 1930s, they were not available to him. He liked to say they belonged to the "old line, silk-stocking crowd," his way of describing the contractors who clus-tered around politicians at that time. He felt that, as a Jew, he was exclu-ded from jobs rou-tinely held

Victor with his good friend Theodore McKeldin at Baltimore Contractors' stag party in December of 1952.

by Christians. "It was a closed club. You couldn't get in with a shoe horn," Victor said years later.

He would contribute heavily to all political candidates and wait to see who emerged as the winner. As a player in a game he thoroughly enjoyed, he was constantly sizing up talent and chances.

In 1935, not long after Victor founded Baltimore Contractors, fate played him a favorable hand. About the time he decided to go after bigger jobs, Victor met a lawyer who appealed to him at first sight. His name was Theodore Roosevelt McKeldin, a gifted speaker with a stentorian voice, a man who instantly made a strong impression on those he met. Eight years older than Victor, he was one of eleven children born in a blue-collar section of South Baltimore. McKeldin, who would go on to be elected mayor twice, then serve eight years as Maryland's governor, was a political unknown in 1935. While both men shared similar family backgrounds, McKeldin was a Republican and Victor a Democrat. Nevertheless, they formed a strong bond.

Frenkil and McKeldin met while on opposite sides of a legal case. Victor was about to be flim-flammed by an elaborate con-artist scheme. A man name Seymour Brooks won his confidence by dangling a large construction job before him. The well orchestrated scheme lured Victor from Baltimore to Keyser, West Virginia, and back. In the end, Victor was to have been stung by cashing a phony $3,000 cashier's check for this man. Victor prudently called his father and asked his advice. Izaak Frenkil, who by then had not much time to live, suggested calling the bank and getting a credit check. Victor did, and the information he discovered resulted in Seymour Brooks' arrest. Victor met him at the bank with two police officers, who took him into custody. Brooks asked for an attorney and was given Ted McKeldin, then a lawyer in his middle thirties. Victor lost very little in the deal and, in the process, got to know McKeldin. In fact, they even split the expenses of what it cost them to tangle with Seymour Brooks.

In the process, Victor became a friend of McKeldin, who was then a rising star. He gave substantial backing to McKeldin in 1939, when he ran unsuccessfully for mayor. He underwrote McKeldin again, in his 1942 race for the State House, when he polled very well but unsuccessfully against the Democrat, Herbert R. O'Conor. The third try was successful and, in 1943, McKeldin was elected Baltimore's mayor. Victor now had a friend in his camp.

A photo dated May 19, 1947, attests to their friendship. Victor and McKeldin are standing in Baltimore's City Hall, their heads turned toward the mayor's official portrait, which had probably just been installed. The photograph is inscribed to Victor: "I'd gladly live this whole life 'thru,' just for the joy of knowing you. You're triple AAA and 14 karat. In my book you are the first page and at the top of the list". McKeldin then signed the photo.

Victor (often with his family) and McKeldin would spend many enjoyable occasions together on the governor's yacht, formerly the Sequoia, President Franklin D. Roosevelt's private boat.

Victor's penchant for politics and parties was firmly entrenched by 1943, when he purchased Wilton, the 32-acre Owings Mills estate in Baltimore County. There he staged lawn parties that are still remembered 60 years later. The invitation to one of the festive events was a picture postcard of Wilton's barn. The event was entitled, "The Last Round-Up". The galas were often held on weekend afternoons. The grass would be freshly cut, the gardens immaculately groomed, the

Victor schmoozing with some of the male guests at a Baltimore Contractors party held at his estate, "Wilton," in Owings Mills in June of 1958.

swimming pool ready. There was always a photographer on hand to record the day. The men appeared dressed in summer silk and linen suits. The women were stylishly outfitted, obviously ready for an elegant afternoon in the country.

These were no ordinary parties. Victor engaged musician Rivers Chambers and his orchestra to stroll among the guests, much in the manner of a society wedding. Children were invited, too. They played in the pool, had their fortunes read by a teller hired for the day or rode on mechanical amusement-park rides Victor brought in.

Margaret Frenkil prepared some of the dishes served — and kept a skillful hostess' eye on the caterer as well. The meal ended with fancy ice creams molded into interesting shapes by the old-line Baltimore firm of Fiske's, a Park Avenue confectioner.

One family story about Wilton centers on a beautiful

Sunday afternoon when the governor's limousine rolled up the driveway. Out popped then-Governor Teddy McKeldin and his wife, Honolulu. The only problem was they had the wrong date. Margaret, ever ready for surprises of this sort, quickly prepared them a meal and everybody had a laugh.

Judge Dulaney Foster, longtime friend of Victor, at a Wilton party.

Wilton's lawn party guests were drawn from the ranks of the legal, political and construction communities — almost anyone whose favor Victor wanted to curry. For decades, he had his secretaries keep scrapbooks full of clippings detailing political tidbits and information about governmental construction programs. These news articles supplied names of people who could benefit Victor — and, as he would feel, vice versa.

Victor's social activities did not end with the summer. For a number of years, he bought a block of seats at the Army-Navy football game in Philadelphia and chartered two Pennsylvania Railroad coaches for his entourage. Those guests were often drawn from the political community. On two occasions he flew a party to the Orange Bowl from Baltimore.

In the winters, his secretaries sent out invitations to his Duck Dinner, a stag affair at the Maryland Club, the men's organization whose members were drawn from Baltimore's socially prominent families. Here he needed a little help from his old colleague and friend, Judge Dulaney Foster, a veteran

Maryland Club member who could open the place, for a night, to Victor, a Jew who never had membership privileges. Judge Foster made the necessary arrangements for the private party, which Victor underwrote.

"I thought I ought to do something for Victor because he was so kind to me," Judge Foster said in 2003, recalling their more than 50 years of friendship.

The choice of the Maryland Club for his dinner appealed to Victor. While he was not a member, he understood the draw a socially restrictive private club had. He also knew that its connections to old money would help assure a good turnout. The event had a selective guest list, focused on Baltimore's and Maryland's top banking and political people, mayors, governors, senators and congressmen who sat at formally appointed tables. Victor was a devotee of terrapin stew, a butter-and-sherry-laced dish that few people ate outside the Maryland Club. (Its laborious preparation requires a specialized knowledge of how to cook this reptile.) Also on the menu would be breast of goose or duck and beaten biscuits. It was an era when French wines were still considered by all to be the world's finest, so Victor's duck dinner always included several wines from the best-known vineyards.

It was a night of speeches, cigars and drinking. Some said it went on too long, but Victor always liked milking such events for the maximum advantage. Even the menu, locally shot game and terrapin stew, went well with the custom of toasting the state and city, many of whose construction projects were now being done by Baltimore Contractors.

After he moved from Wilton and settled at the Marylander Apartments in the city, he threw an annual Preakness party. As late as May, 1997, when he was 88 years, he invited prominent attorney and Oriole owner Peter Angelos, former Congress member Helen Delich Bentley, Baltimore budget director Charles L. Benton, the treasurer of the United States, Mary Ellen Withrow, former U.S. Senator Daniel Brewster, city redevelopment official M. Jay Brodie, state comptroller Louis Goldstein, attorney Francis Burch Jr., Dr. Calvin Burnett, president of Coppin State College, John Carroll, editor of *The Baltimore Sun*, James Fisher, president of Towson University, Maryland attorney General, J. Joseph Curran Jr., Annapolis Mayor Alfred Hopkins, the President of the University of Maryland, William Kirwan, and a host of judges and their spouses, among many other names that appeared with frequency in the news. Not all these people would accept Victor's invitation, but many did. Many returned year after year, long after they had retired from their professional lives.

In his recollections of 1940s politics in Baltimore — and what it took to land a construction contract — Victor was blunt. He recalled having to pay $10,000 (a huge sum in those days) under the table to municipal officials to be considered for concrete work to build a Baltimore & Ohio Railroad high-

The Baltimore & Ohio Railroad overpass built by Baltimore Contractors on Erdman Avenue, northeast Baltimore. Victor admitted that, to get the job, he had to pay a fee of $10,000 — which he did gladly.

The stadium at the University of Maryland, on 6 February 1952, built by Baltimore Contractors.

way overpass along Erdman Avenue in Northeast Baltimore. He got the job and was so pleased that he inscribed his name in the wet concrete.

In the mid-1940s he watched the political games being

The first completed bent of the Chesapeake Bay Bridge is inspected by a team including William Preston Lane, governor of Maryland.

played at Baltimore's City Hall and didn't like what he observed. He was not getting the construction jobs he wanted because he felt the city's chief engineer, the director of the Department of Public Works, was not looking favorably on Baltimore Contractors. In an account he left before his death, Victor said it cost him $25,000 to change this situation. How he changed it was never clear, although he said he had a meeting with "two brothers" in City Hall.

Early in 1948, *The Sun* and other newspapers reported that Mayor Thomas J. D'Alesandro, Jr., had appointed a new city engineer, Paul L. Holland, a graduate of the Naval Academy who had put in many years at the state's Public Service Commission. Newspaper editorials lauded the appointment of the highly accomplished professional.

Victor was now satisfied. Baltimore Contractors began to get its share of the city work — and there was plenty to go around.

Victor's years of political hustling served him well in the 1950s and 1960s when both the city and state embarked on major public-works projects.

Among the multi-million-dollar jobs he won was the contract to build the causeway on the Eastern Shore side of the Chesapeake Bay Bridge; an extensive remodeling of the old Baltimore City Hospitals building; the University of Maryland Stadium, Field House, dormitories and fraternity houses; cottages at Crownsville State Hospital; Frostburg State College dormitories; the Baltimore Civic Center; the Maryland World's Fair Pavilion in Flushing, N.Y.; the Baltimore Polytechnic and Western High Schools; and the Edward Garmatz Federal Building in downtown Baltimore.

Victor's political aspirations and associations were never limited to Maryland. He was drawn to national figures as well.

The race track in San Juan, Puerto Rico, one of Baltimore Contractors' early ventures outside the continental United States (shown in January 1957).

One of these was Republican presidential candidate Wendell Willkie, whom he met in Baltimore in 1940, first at a private meeting with backers in June of that year and again, in late October, just before Willkie was soundly defeated by Franklin D. Roosevelt. Victor's personality meshed with the Midwesterner Willkie in the few hours they spent together. (It was during this encounter that Victor's habit of folding dollar bills for friends was born. He had been given a dollar bill folded by campaign staffers into a "W" that was a custom of Willkie. This, of course, would become the Frenkil trademark.) When candidate Willkie died in 1944, Victor remained loyal to the family and hosted W. Frederick Willkie, the candidate's brother, in Baltimore when he gave a speech before the Advertising Club in April 1947.

In the presidential election of 1948, Victor campaigned for Harry S. Truman and was rewarded with an appointment to the draft board. In 1951, the president placed him on the Federal Assay Commission, a post that required him to visit the U.S. Mint and verify that coinage was being made according to the rules. He and Margaret also traveled to Philadelphia on July 14, 1948, for a portion of the nominating convention held there. This would not be Victor's last trip to a national political convention.

He made it a point to be on good terms with Maryland's congressional delegation. His jammed appointment logs of this period are filled with luncheons and meetings, most often in Baltimore's downtown hotels, the Emerson, the Lord Baltimore and the Southern, but not infrequently in Washington at the Mayflower and Statler. Victor was learning to spread his wings and work the Washington political circuit. By all accounts, he liked it very much.

Victor's contracting work was now growing beyond the mid-Atlantic region. In February of 1960, Victor charged impetuously into a business deal that would reach all the way into a governor's mansion, and by extension, Washington, D.C. He gambled on a project he didn't fully understand, lost a fortune, then spent the next three or four years doggedly trying to recoup the money he lost.

He ventured out of his usual orbit (he had built some air-base buildings in Spain where his son, Leonard, ran the operation, and a race track in San Juan, Puerto Rico, but most of his projects were close to home) and bid successfully on the Houma Tunnel in Louisiana, a highway tube under the inter-coastal waterway in Terrebone Parish. Victor sent his son, Victor Jr., on this three-year assignment, where he endured heat, mosquitoes, prejudice and obstacles as difficult as they were unexpected.

In the process of digging, the workers encountered a sub-merged petrified cypress forest, which had to be dug out at great expense, a cost Victor had not foreseen and which was not included in his winning bid. Victor sought financial

Victor (Bruz) Frenkil, Jr., office manager of the Houma tunnel project, by a petrified stump. Baltimore Contractors ran into an unexpected petrified forest under water, causing overruns of $1.2 million that were never repaid.

redress. In the process of negotiating considerable cost overruns, he ingratiated himself to Governor Jimmie Davis, who first gained national attention as a singer and had a big hit with his version of "You Are My Sunshine".

At first, Victor had trouble making inroads into the Deep South and, specifically, the Louisiana governor's mansion. Once again, he used his savvy and his charm. He sent a bouquet of roses to gain access to Ann Fagg, the governor's secretary, a woman he'd heard might help him. Once flattered, she accepted his invitation to dinner at Antoine's in New Orleans. That evening she insisted that the governor's appointment calendar was booked, but suggested that, if Victor just showed up early one morning, he just might run into the state's chief executive. Victor asked around and learned that Governor Davis was passionate about dogs, especially hunting retrievers. So he bought him one.

Little by little, Victor and the Governor became friends. Victor stayed in contact with the secretary and, years later, flew her up to one of his Preakness parties. At that event, she met George P. Mahoney, a paving contractor and perennial political aspirant. They were later married.

The tunnel project was not nearly as happy as that marriage. The tunnel, which opened in 1962, remains busy 44 years later. Its complicated construction involved vast unseen costs. And the overruns of about $1.2 million for the unanticipated costs of the Houma Tunnel were never paid to Baltimore Contractors.

Victor, who savored the challenge of building the tunnel, also enjoyed the pursuit of what he considered a proper payment of what it cost him. He wined and dined Ray W. Burgess, a Louisiana official who headed the state's construction program, on several occasions in 1963. Despite his remarkable skills in bending people in his direction, Victor was denied the full cost of removing the petrified cypress trees. To cover this loss, he was forced to sell his beloved Marylander Apartments, which had been an excellent source of income.

While Victor was happy to play the political game with both parties to make sure he was with a winner, he was essentially a Democrat. The presidential election of 1960 proved to be fascinating for him. After eight years of the Eisenhower administration, it appeared that the Democrats had a strong chance to return to the White House. Victor kept on eye on the convention in Los Angeles. The delegates nominated John F. Kennedy and Lyndon B. Johnson, who went on to win in what was an unusually close election that fall.

Maryland's governor Marvin Mandel recalled Victor's early friendship with the Kennedy-Johnson team. "Victor was always a contributor to the Democratic Party and I recall him meeting them. He had access to John Kennedy, although not nearly as much as he ultimately had with Lyndon Johnson."

Governor Mandel assessed Victor: "He was always very active in Maryland politics through his relationships and friendships. He was not a political leader in the sense of being elected. He was independent, very smart and knew just which buttons to push. To this day (2003), I carry a dollar bill he folded with my initials many years ago".

Victor was traditionally a generous contributor to all political campaigns. By 1963, his appointment book was filled with entries noting trips to the Democratic Party's national headquarters in Washington. They also reveal repeated meetings, lunches, early morning sessions, as well as train trips to New York, with Walter Jenkins, Lyndon Johnson's chief aide (who was soon to become one of the most powerful men in Washington). Victor was not one to give up a fight easily, especially when significant money was involved, and he still had hopes of recovering his Houma Tunnel losses. Victor's personality often connected well with political figures who, through their hard work, had climbed the ranks. Jenkins and Victor hit it off at once. Victor, as ever, mixed entertaining with business (to him they were one and the same) and was soon a trusted friend of Jenkins. Jenkins, of course, could draw upon the contacts he had made in his 25 years of work with Johnson and open doors along the way.

As the 1964 presidential campaign was winding down, Victor was caught off guard by a breaking news story concerning his new Washington ally. Jenkins, a married man, had been arrested and charged with indecent sexual behavior in a Washington YMCA men's room. The story rocked the country because of Jenkins' insider status, and general popularity, in Washington. Victor initially thought the story was a Republican setup, but changed his mind after he heard from Deke DeLoach, an FBI contact, that the arrest was legitimate.

Victor had been campaigning hard for Lyndon Johnson that summer and had generated about $30,000 by folding LBJ dollar bills at political gatherings. Victor rounded up the cash to help his friend Jenkins get through what was to prove an extremely difficult period. As a political realist, Johnson, now furious at his once-trusted assistant, had to distance himself from Jenkins immediately.

Margaret Frenkil stayed with Mrs. Jenkins for several days during a court hearing. Meanwhile, Walter Jenkins checked into a hospital to avoid reporters. Soon the couple found themselves abandoned by all their Washington friends. They decided to seek seclusion in Puerto Rico. Victor stayed in close contact with them, helping in every way he could. In the confusion of helping them get out of Washington as quietly as possible, Victor literally led them onto the airplane and into their seats. Continuing to converse with them, he realized that he had no ticket and, of course, no baggage. While the captain fumed, he made a quick deal with a stewardess to run inside the airport and buy him passage. He then flew to San Juan with the Jenkins and stayed with them until they got settled. They checked into the Hilton and he treated the couple to dinner at its rooftop restaurant. He danced with Mrs. Jenkins and told as many jokes as he could remember. Then he realized that Margaret had no idea where he was.

He attempted to call home, but couldn't get through. He told his problem to the orchestra leader, who knew how to get things done. In a few minutes, he was telling Margaret "I'll be home a little late. I'm at the Hilton in San Juan, Puerto Rico". Victor caught a plane at 1AM and was back at his desk the next morning. Jenkins eventually recovered and opened a consulting business in Austin, Texas. Victor signed up as a client and paid him handsomely for his influence and advice regarding construction jobs for the next several years. As late as 1970, they sunk money into a hotel resort, the Casa de Pesca, at Acapulco, Mexico. Their financial dealings continued through the late 1970s.

Victor's stock with Lyndon Johnson soared after the 1964 election. A letter dated November 21, 1964, arrived at Victor's 711 South Central Avenue office only weeks after Johnson's victory at the polls over Arizona Republican Senator Barry Goldwater. "It was your financial help that enabled the President to so effectively carry his case to the American people," wrote Richard Maguire, treasurer of the Democratic National Committee. Victor received a personal invitation to a prime seat at the upcoming inauguration as a member of the President's Club, a group of campaign contributors. Over the next two months, a flurry of letters went back and forth from Baltimore Contractors to the various arrangement committees in Washington.

Victor decided to take an entourage to the capital, and the Frenkil party at the presidential inauguration assumed the proportions of a wedding. He called in a number of obligations. Senator Daniel Brewster arranged for extra hotel rooms. Victor contacted Maryland's then-Governor, Millard Tawes, to ask why the state had not entered a float in the inaugural parade. (A note in Virginia Lambrow's handwriting says she was told the state had no money for a float.) He hired a pair of limousines to leave from the Marylander Apartments, and had a

Victor hired a carriage to open Baltimore's annual Flower Mart with Mayor William Donald Schaefer, Marian Hecht and Margaret.

typed agenda prepared. There were carefully prepared notes about which events were formal and whether the ladies were to wear long dresses. Virginia even typed which afternoon functions required the women to wear a hat. Baltimore Contractors wound up paying more than $3,000 for the excursion to Washington, a tab Victor never flinched at paying, given the access and exposure the events afforded.

Their party included Baltimore Mayor McKeldin, who, though a Republican, all but openly endorsed Johnson. Victor's long-time friend James Swartz, his business associates Leonard Hudson, Albert Backhaus and Virginia Lambrow, and his son, Leonard Frenkil, and their wives or guests attended.

It was a busy January for Margaret and Victor Frenkil. Not only did they attend inaugural concerts, banquets and receptions as well as the actual swearing-in ceremony and parade, they were also invited to a cocktail party in honor of Texas Governor John Connally, a man widely viewed as a serious

Lady Bird Johnson sent this photo to Victor with her inscription underneath that reads, "For Victor Frenkil with warm affection over the years, Lady Bird Johnson, May 1994".

contender in upcoming presidential contests.

Victor turned on his charm with the newly inaugurated president, even having his inaugural address reproduced in miniature booklet form, then mailing it to every public official he knew, with, of course, the name "Victor Frenkil" imprinted on it. President Johnson returned the favors. The two became friends. By the year's end a personal invitation came inviting Victor to the White House for a one-on-one session with LBJ. The meeting took place just before Christmas of 1965. The president presented Victor with a Texas-style hat. Victor had folded dollars to read "Merry Xmas and a Happy New Year" and had them mounted on green felt. Accompanying him was his faithful secretary, Virginia Lambrow. Photographers snapped pictures to document the occasion.

Victor cemented his relationship with the Oval Office by cultivating a friendship with Mildred Stegall, the president's confidential secretary (after all, the secretary route worked well with Governor Jimmie Davis). What happened when they befriended this White House doorkeeper was amazing. Virginia, though her connections with Mrs. Stegall, was able to get the president on the phone almost any time.

More than one of Victor's Baltimore associates were dumbfounded when Victor, at his desk on South Central Avenue, was able to get through to the president. This access, and the familiarities the two men exchanged, added mightily to the perception of Victor's political clout. A letter from Miss Stegall records the late-night conversations between the Jewish contractor from Baltimore and the President of the United States.

The friendship between the two secretaries continues after four decades. Miss Stegall still corresponds with Virginia Lambrow.

Victor shamelessly used his connections with the President to impress his Baltimore colleagues. Baltimore mayor and later Maryland governor, William Donald Schaefer, recalled a day in the 1960s when he visited Victor's office in search of a job. He recalled being ushered into Victor's big office at the top of the steps.

"Before long Vic was calling out to Virginia, 'Get President Johnson on the phone'. And she did. Then he was calling out, 'Get Admiral Ben Moreell on the phone'. And she did. Now I was really impressed. I thought that day he was a real hot patootie," Schaefer said in 2003 in his office as the state's comptroller. ("Patootie" was a word common in Baltimore slang at the time, meaning "sweetheart" or "hot stuff".)

Schaefer also assessed Victor's reputation in Maryland politics. "His reputation was to be a little careful around him. He'd bid low on a project and get you on all the change orders. That was the reputation. I never found this to be true. He was in fact a high-class builder."

Schaefer continued: "I think Victor liked to play games with people. If his reputation was a little bit off, he liked that. It gave him an edge he enjoyed. What he really liked was being a big deal, taking a big gang of people on a bus to Pimlico for the Preakness. Or at a restaurant, always reaching for the check. And he loved having his name in the papers, good or bad. That was important to him.

"He was smart. He could think things out. When you were with him, he put you at ease. You felt comfortable," Schaefer said.

President Johnson chose not to run for a second term in 1968. Victor continued to drop him notes and also spent time with him, his secretary and former Texas Governor John Connally at the 1968 Democratic National Convention held at Chicago. When the former president died in January, 1973, Victor had a Loyola College Jesuit, Father Daniel McGuire, offer a Mass for his friend. In turn, when Victor died in 2000, both Lady Bird Johnson and Mildred Stegall wrote condolence letters to the Frenkil family.

Victor never forgot his friends. Through Virginia Lambrow, he wrote to Lady Bird Johnson and sent her gifts, including a rustic rocking chair hand-made of tree branches. Mrs. Johnson expressed her appreciation for the chair, which was photographed when a home-decorating magazine published a feature story on her Stonewall, Texas, residence. Lady Bird sent the magazine to Victor, who, in turn showed it to his friends. From time to time he dispatched a refrigerated box of Chesapeake Bay steamed crabs to her as well.

After Johnson left office, Victor also kept his eye squarely focused on potential candidate John Connally, whom he had known for more than a decade.

Victor got to know John Connally well in the 1960s when Connally, then a Democrat, was Secretary of the Navy and Victor won contracts at the Naval Academy and along the Potomac River docks in Washington. Victor immediately

Formal opening of the Marylander Apartments. From left: Governor Theodore R. McKeldin, Mrs. and Mayor Tommy D'Alesandro, Senator George M. Radcliffe, (unknown), Victor, Jennie (Victor's mother), and Margaret Frenkil.

Baltimore Contractors built the Children's Hospital in Philadelphia, shown here in May of 1974.

Grain bins built by Baltimore Contractors for the Western Maryland Railway Company in Port Covington, shown in April of 1944.

Victor's beloved Marylander at St. Paul Street and University Parkway in Baltimore, which he built, lived in and owned until forced to sell.

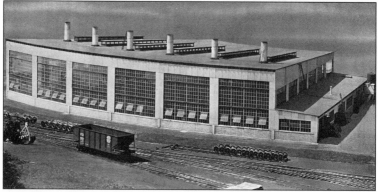

The Western Maryland Railway roundhouse, in Port Covington, Maryland, built by Baltimore Contractors.

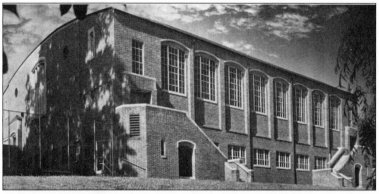

Baltimore Contractors built the Towson State Teachers College gymnasium.

became cozy with Connally and arranged for his son, Leonard, to move to Texas one summer and work as summer campaign help for Connally — as an undercover agent in his opponent's political campaign, a nice bit of political intrigue.

Connally jumped from the Democratic Party and joined Richard Nixon's cabinet as Secretary of the Treasury, a move that annoyed Victor, who would have preferred that Connally remain a Democrat. The two men knew each other fairly well. The tone of Victor's communications suggests a certain intimacy. Victor wrote to Connally several times in the 1970s, including a May 17, 1979 letter in which he told Connally: "I probably would have prevailed upon you to not cross over the Democratic line. Of course, President Johnson, Mildred Stegall and Walter Jenkins were quite disappointed and unhappy when you made that decision".

Connally was also being touted by the media as a possible Nixon running mate in 1972. Victor thought this a good idea and wrote to him on January 11, 1971: "Since I was with you in Chicago when the last Presidential candidacy was concluded, maybe, Lord willing, I can again be with you when the next Democratic Presidential candidate is selected. You are quite a formidable person for the highest office of the land. You should go to the post". Just to keep his old friend up on his thoughts, Victor also sent a blind copy of his letter to fellow-Texan Walter Jenkins, who was also most likely feeding Victor his own impressions of Connally's prospects.

In August of that year, Victor sounded much like the Republican that Connally had become.

Victor had Virginia Lambrow telephone the Treasury Secretary. A transcript records that Virginia spoke to Cynthia McMahon, Connally's personal secretary. Victor recommended the suspension of the Taft-Hartley law and the elimination of minimum wage in government contracts. "In the case of unions which continue to strike, injunctions and fines against the unions, and the union leaders, should be invoked immediately."

In October, Victor wrote Connally, this time to offer use of a Chesapeake Bay retreat he owned, Barren Island. "You will find the Island the most restful, relaxing place on the Eastern seaboard…it is situated at the mouth of the Chesapeake Bay, and it would be quite restful — but most important, no telephones. If an emergency should arise, we have radio communication." Connally politely declined.

One of Victor's most energetic political excursions was the Maryland governor's race of 1966. His close ally, J. Millard Tawes, who followed McKeldin in the Maryland governor's mansion, had served two terms. Governor Tawes rewarded Victor with a seat on the state panel that oversaw colleges and universities. At the higher-education board meetings, he sat and folded dollar bills as he offered his opinion on the subjects at hand.

At the height of their friendship, the following story circulated. Governor Tawes was admitted to University of Maryland Hospital in downtown Baltimore for a routine operation. As he came out of the anesthetic, he looked up and saw a man dressed in surgical scrubs and a face mask. Then he recognized the eyes: It was Victor, who had talked his way into the operating room.

Victor liked being on friendly, first-name terms with Maryland's chief executives. In 1966, as Governor Tawes was

Vic at a job with Louis Goldstein, Maryland's longest-serving public servant. Goldstein wrote on the picture: "Best wishes to Victor Frenkil, a great buddy".

about to leave office, Victor had no intentions of letting that patiently acquired influence evaporate. After all, it meant certain perks, such as helping with the appointments of district and circuit-court judges. Victor had his friends on the bench. He was close to Anselm Sodaro, Baltimore's chief judge, and Dulaney Foster, a close ally who served as president of the Marylander Apartments, the building Victor constructed from 1950-1951 (and where he lived for nearly half a century). He was also friendly with judges Robert Murphy and Robert Watts (one of the state's first African-Americans to sit on the bench).

"There wasn't a judge appointed to the bench under McKeldin and Tawes that Victor didn't have approval power over," said attorney George McManus, who handled legal work for Baltimore Contractors.

Victor surveyed the 1966 field of gubernatorial candidates and joined up with Thomas Finan, the state's attorney general who had been on friendly terms with the Tawes forces. The two hit it off well; Finan's running mates, Francis "Bill" Burch in the attorney-general slot and Louis Goldstein for comptroller, were also Victor's pals.

Tom Finan was from Cumberland, 150 miles west of Baltimore. He was not so well known in the more populous parts of the state and needed voter recognition. In addition to his financial underwriting of Finan's campaign, Victor lent his private plane, ordinarily used for going to distant Baltimore Contractors' work sites. He also called on his friend, advertising executive Tony Weir, for help when the Finan campaign got into trouble.

The problem was not Victor's support, but the disarray in which the Democratic Party found itself. That year, four major candidates declared in the primary: Finan, attorney Clarence W. Miles, paving contractor George P. Mahoney and congressman-at-large Carlton Sickles.

Mahoney, who caught the public's attention and fears with the racially charged slogan, "Your home is your castle. Protect it", outpolled the other three. Sickles ran second, Finan placed third and Miles took the fourth spot. There were bitter in-house feuds during the election. Campaign staffers recall that if Clarence Miles, a Baltimore attorney, had turned his support over to Finan, Finan would have won. Instead, Miles ran last. He and Victor were not political allies.

When the election results were tallied September 13, 1966, the results were a disaster for Victor and, in a way, for the entire country. Candidate Finan, a highly respected and able man, spent the day at one of Victor's business subsidiaries, Jarvis Steel (which had been purchased by his son, Victor). It was a dismal night. Finan ran third, behind Mahoney and Sickles. Yet running mates Louis Goldstein and Bill Burch won the primary and the general elections.

Mahoney, who always ran but never won, went on to run against, and be defeated by, a little-known Republican candidate, Spiro T. Agnew — someone Finan would have likely defeated with ease in the general election, given the exposure that the Democratic party could have achieved for him.

Agnew, who in 1966 was the Baltimore County chief executive, was so little regarded that Victor declined to meet him — not something he often did in the game of politics he so loved. Instead, he sent his loyal corporate secretary, Virginia Lambrow, to the front entrance of Baltimore Contractors on South Central Avenue when candidate Agnew came to introduce himself and solicit campaign support.

Victor did not even suggest bringing Agnew up the stairs to his private office, as was his usual custom. This brushoff proved to be one of his worst political mistakes (and very unlike the person who so assiduously wooed both sides of the political spectrum throughout his career).

Victor later felt this failure to recognize Agnew cost him a political friendship after Agnew was tapped by Richard Nixon as his 1968 running mate. Victor and Agnew were never to become close political buddies. While they shared no animosity, the close personal ties and the kind of familiarity and friendship that Victor liked to cultivate were just not possible.

Governor Marvin Mandel, the former speaker of the House, who took office in January 1969, recalled an incident with Victor. "I received an invitation to the Baltimore Contractors' Christmas party at the Belvedere. I didn't know if I could make it. So Victor kept calling me and calling me, asking if I would come. I finally agreed with the stipulation that I could stay only ten minutes."

Marvin Mandel entered the Belvedere ballroom that December night, only to have Victor usher him to the podium and ask him to say a few words. "I thought for a minute, and knowing Victor's reputation for cost overruns on a project, I heartily congratulated his employees on winning the largest contract the state had awarded to that time — the construction of the O'Conor office building on Preston Street. Then, in front of everyone, I said 'Victor has given me his word there would be no additional claims or additional funds needed'."

The governor then made his way down the corridor to the elevator, while Victor dashed to keep up with him, mumbling, "What do you mean?"

Governor Mandel said he got a laugh out of the encounter, but was well aware that Victor "knew his work," adding, "He could analyze a state project".

Victor could always count on Maryland's longtime comptroller, Louis Goldstein, as a friend. And a powerful and lengthy friendship it proved to be.

Goldstein, who held office for so many years that he was the state's longest-serving elected official, was an extremely popular person, who loved the game of politics. A distinctive speaker, he turned down few invitations to open schools, shopping centers and picnic groves. He liked meeting people as much as Victor and was much respected for his knowledge of Maryland's history. He also enjoyed enormous popularity and perhaps made more public appearances daily than Victor Frenkil.

Victor and Louis met in the 1940s. By 1950, the Southern Marylander was taking Victor and Victor Jr. duck hunting on his property in Calvert County.

"While we were waiting for ducks and standing in a blind, Louie said he was thinking of running for comptroller," Victor Jr. recalled. "My father on the spot said he'd back him and contribute to him." Victor Jr. also recalled that they didn't bag any ducks, and that Goldstein always wanted Victor to buy trees from his extensive landholdings.

It was Goldstein who, along with some other friends, sold Victor Barren Island, the remote lower Chesapeake Bay island in Dorchester County. The island, which had a landing strip, had been owned by the Consolidated Engineering Company and had a lodge constructed from parts of the old Caswell Hotel, torn down in the mid-1920s to make way for the Lord Baltimore. Erosion washed much of the island away, including the lodge. Victor found his Chesapeake Bay domain costly because of the constant bulkheading that was required. He ultimately sold the place.

One outcome of the primary of 1966 was a cementing of Victor's longstanding relationship with Louis Goldstein. The two were close political allies. Victor invited Goldstein to services at Har Sinai Congregation. The comptroller was also a frequent guest at Victor's parties.

"No matter how busy he was, Louie would always drop whatever he was doing and answer the telephone when Victor called," said Kenneth B. Yekstat, a state trooper who was Goldstein's driver. "Louie wouldn't do that for anybody else."

Victor was not in good health when Goldstein died in 1998. Victor Jr. drove his father to the funeral in Upper

Marlboro. They were late and the parking lot was overflowing. Victor told his son to drive up to the front door. There he nodded at a state trooper, who instantly recognized him. Then came the words Victor had been accustomed to hearing for decades: "Hello, Mr. Frenkil. Park it right there by the door. I'll keep an eye on it for you".

Victor's charm and political influence still worked their magic, even at his advanced age.

VIII. Fighting
City Hall

"As though to be Jewish weren't trouble enough..."
Saul Bellow

B y the end of the 1960s, the rules of going after government contracts were being rewritten. Victor, who virtually wrote the rules of the older system, ploughed headlong into a situation that fractured his reputation and, for once in his life, terrified him. He, his name and his reputation were spread over the pages of *The New York Times* and *Washington Post* for nearly nine months. He even made *Life Magazine*.

By this time, he had been in the contracting business for 40 years. Controversy was nothing new to him; some of his friends said he thrived on it. Construction was a tough game he played offensively, often oblivious to the financial penalties attached. He thought he knew all the players, or at least knew how to win their confidence and put out any fires along the way.

"He wasn't a crook, but he went to the edge. I don't think he ever made a bribe. I don't think he ever did anything that falls within the realm of illegal practice," said Mathias J. "Matt" DeVito, who met Victor when both sat on a state

117

board that oversaw Maryland's colleges and universities. DeVito, younger by 30 years, was then an attorney and about to become president of the Rouse Company, the developer of Maryland's Columbia and numerous shopping centers. He fell under the spell of Victor's charm. They remained friends for the rest of Victor's life.

Matt DeVito soon found himself Victor's unpaid advisor and the recipient of hundreds of phone calls. Victor sought, and occasionally heeded, Matt DeVito's sage advice. DeVito, a savvy and articulate individual, spent hours, as he put it, "trying to keep Victor from being Victor" in what developed into a tight spot that could have led to a federal prison sentence.

"Underlying his aggressive behavior was this issue of Victor's being Jewish. He saw a monolithic class of people, all Gentiles. I think he felt, 'How else am I going to get things done if I don't attack the system with everything I've got?'" DeVito said. "Victor knew he was not going to get certain types of work, like hospitals (run by boards, often of one ethnic persuasion). He could also concoct self-serving stories, situations he believed to be true."

So Victor often bid on government contracts where he felt he had influence because of his financial contributions, friendships and influence over elected officials and so many people around them. He fervently believed, in his own words, that Victor Frenkil was a "Jew Boy" who had to fight hard and tough in a silk-stocking world in which the odds were against him, and the boards of directors and corporate officers, all largely Gentile, had it in for persons of the Jewish religion.

"He was an exceedingly complex person. There was a hyper-activity around his style that was coupled with a paranoia about his being this Jew Boy — that was his word — and nobody giving him work," DeVito said.

"If he had an objective, he would attack it five different ways. With five different people working for him, not knowing they had all been hired to do the same thing. It would all be very counterproductive," DeVito recalled. "Then he would start calling, every night, every day. Fortunately he had a short attention span and he wouldn't talk too long."

In 1966, during the administration of his friend Lyndon Johnson, Victor bid on and won an $11-million contract to construct an underground parking garage for the Sam Rayburn Office Building on Capitol Hill in Washington. Victor's work crew ran into unusually difficult and unexpected problems with soil conditions and other issues. When the job was over, the company submitted a $5-million claim for these unanticipated costs to the Office of the Capitol Architect. Victor also hired Steptoe and Johnson, a well-respected Washington legal firm, to handle the claim.

Victor's campaign to be paid all (or at least part) of this $5 million claim embroiled him in the legal battle of his life.

"What happened was the Members of the House didn't want it to come out how much the construction costs were for a single parking space. They wanted the convenience of the parking near their offices, but they didn't want the per-space cost to ever be reported in the press," said his attorney Jack Jones, who became one of several lawyers Victor hired. "At that time, how would it look if it came out that members of Congress were parking in spaces that cost the price of a small house?"

Victor Jr. recalls his father bristling at what Congress wanted to appropriate for its own use. It rattled his sense of proper use of public funds, but, having won the contract, he did the work — and presented the bill. Victor Jr. said his father never imagined the furor that bill would bring on. He did think it was a good idea to expose how much was being spent on a project whose financial value was open to question.

Seeking compensation for the overruns, Victor met with George Stewart, an elderly engineer who held the office of Capitol Architect (and who would die in 1970). The two tangled verbally. And the Capitol Architect rejected the claim, as did others in his office. Victor, as was his custom, called in all his elected allies in Maryland. As an inveterate string-puller, he began to call in the Capitol Hill IOUs he had won through political donations and special favors. He used whatever influence he had.

Victor's normal practice would have been to go to the individual who was in charge and somehow, using whatever it took, he'd get something back for whatever loss Baltimore Contractors suffered. The Office of the Capitol Architect was not a single person; directly and indirectly, it answered to all of Congress, whose members wanted to keep the lid on what it cost to run their offices and park their cars. And it would not look good if it came out that Congress was spending $12,600 for each parking space.

Ironically, Victor almost didn't get the job. He initially lost out to a pair of New York companies, Brookfield and Baylor, who were turned down because they submitted a performance bond that was too low. The companies corrected the bond within 24 hours after the bids were opened, but by then Capitol Architect George Stewart accepted the lowest bid of $11.7 million from Baltimore Contractors. The New York firms took the matter to U.S. District Court, but Victor's bid stood.

By the fall of 1965, when the garage was rising out of the ground, Victor's work crews were experiencing problems with unforeseen issues. Specifically, Victor claimed there were unan-

Looking northeast over the site of the underground parking garage for the Sam Rayburn Office Building on Capitol Hill in Washington in May of 1965, the job that almost buried Victor Frenkil and Baltimore Contractors. This was probably the gravest crisis of his life.

ticipated soil conditions present at the site in Washington. The government countered by claiming there were sufficient data available to make the soil conditions known. The garage issue played out over a full decade and was not settled until 1974.

Victor made four complaints in his suit:

"1. That subsurface soil conditions differed materially from what was described in the contract.

"2. That a nearby sewer had caused a construction problem that had not been indicated in the project.

"3. That the government forced work beyond the terms of the contract by requiring excavation slopes steeper than necessary, by requiring an excessive number of tests to determine the strength of earth anchors and by requiring extra supervisory

121

personnel.

"4. That the government caused delays by failing to make the site available on time, by withholding required approvals of construction procedures for 'unreasonable' periods and by taking too long approving construction drawings." (*The Baltimore Sun*, 8 October 1974).

At the height of pressing his case, Victor sought and obtained a remarkable letter of support, signed by both of Maryland's senators as well as the state's members in the House of Representatives. A letter from Maryland's congressional delegation was written dated 18 February 1969. It was addressed to John W. McCormack, Emanuel Celler and William C. Cramer, all members of the House Office Commission.

"During the past two years, I have been interested in having the disputes between the contractor and the Architect of the Capitol resolved. Most recently, I have participated in two conferences on the above-noted claim between the contractor and the representatives of the Architect of the Capitol. This claim involves exceedingly complicated engineering and solids questions....It is quite apparent that the Architect of the Capitol is relying exclusively on his consultants, who, in fact, are the ones who made the original decisions and designs which are the gravamens of the controversy. It seems apparent that a decision was made some time in the past to deny the contractor's claim, with no real effort to direct discussions to resolve fundamental soils and engineering issues."

"It was an amazing letter, signed by the entire Maryland delegation. It showed Victor's connections in Washington," said DeVito.

Victor didn't stop at the Maryland delegation. He also contacted his old friends from Louisiana, Senator Russell Long and House Member Hale Boggs, who was minority whip.

Coincidentally, Victor had done $11,000 worth of renovation work to the Boggs' residence in Bethesda in 1966, long before the claim for extra money was filed — something that would be mentioned with obvious innuendo in many newspaper reports.

"You have to remember Victor was one of the old-time contractors. He flew by the seat of his pants. He did deals with the top guys and started work fast. He would often be out on the street, working without a contract," said John N. Jones, one of his attorneys, whom Victor later tapped to be an executive of his company.

The letter, and whatever pressure Victor applied at the Capitol Architect's Office, brought on a federal investigation in 1969. The man leading that investigation was himself an odd adversary for Victor — a man who had worked on his behalf as a lawyer in the firm Victor had been relying upon for more than 30 years. He was Stephen H. Sachs, who was then the federal prosecutor for the state of Maryland. Educated at Haverford and Yale, liberal, bright and long an advocate for the little guy, Sachs too shared Victor's penchant for politics and would, years later, be talked about as a candidate for governor. In the 1960s, as federal prosecutor for Maryland, he was investigating political corruption and was, in fact, on a roll, having brought down Thomas Johnson, a Maryland legislator convicted of bribe-taking.

In the early months of 1969, Sachs called a federal grand jury in Baltimore and subpoenaed Baltimore Contractors' records, appointment books and business records. He also called Victor, his corporate secretary Virginia Lambrow and Jerry Jarosinski, among others. Victor and his associates were subjected to hours and hours of questions.

Word spread around town that Sachs was going to come at

Victor Frenkil with the full weight of the federal government's investigative arms and machinery.

"If the federal government pursues you, it is awesome. This was a very scary thing — FBI agents rough-handling you, in a threatening way. They can interview your employees and your subcontractors and threaten jail time if they don't talk. As a citizen, it was a frightening thing to see how the federal government can investigate you. When Sachs subpoenaed Victor's records, Victor became seriously scared," DeVito said.

"I'm sure Sachs sincerely thought Victor was a crook. Sachs had the conviction there was a very bad man involved in the public life of Baltimore," DeVito said.

"Victor was fighting for his life," said William Hundley, the Washington attorney who was eventually called in on the case. "He'd call me at three or four in the morning. And no matter where I was, with a time difference, he'd get it mixed up."

Even his friend, Washington-insider Walter Jenkins, advised Victor that he could not influence a federal proceeding. He told Victor there was nothing anybody could do when a grand jury and federal attorney had started an investigation.

Before long, the story of the investigation was public news. The story broke in a copyrighted page-one feature in *The Washington Post* on the morning of Saturday, 30 August 1969, in the middle of a sleepy Labor Day weekend. It was headlined "Jury Investigates Sen. Long, Brewster," a reference to the senators from Louisiana and Maryland.

The lengthy article said that a federal grand jury was "investigating allegations that two United States senators (took) bribes to influence a government contract".

The Washington Post's story further said, "The case upon which the grand jury is expending much of its attention involves allegations that Brewster and Long shared a bribe for

exerting pres-
sure to get
extra costs
approved for
e x t e n s i v e
underground
parking facili-
ties recently
built for the
House of Rep-
resentatives".
Several para-
graphs down, it
i d e n t i f i e d
Victor Frenkil
as the Balti-

House Majority Whip and long-time friend Hale Boggs, who autographed this photo: "To Victor Frenkil from his friend Hale Boggs M.C."

more contractor seeking additional money to reimburse him for added, but unauthorized, expenses on the garage construction. Although the story never said so, it led the reader to believe that Victor was proffering cash bribes to the senators, both of whom he knew well.

Baltimore's three papers immediately picked up the story from *The Post*, as did numerous other U.S. dailies. A firestorm of coverage blazed away for the next ten months, perhaps climaxed by a January 1970 *Life Magazine* article mentioning Victor Frenkil, but focusing on attorney and Washington-insider Nathan Voloshen (to whom Victor had paid a thoroughly legal $20,000 retaining fee). It spoke of Voloshen's role with the House of Representatives' Speaker, John W. McCormack, who himself was being pummeled with criticism for the way he ran his office.

The first wave of news stories focused on the two well-known and popular Louisiana politicians Victor met in conjunction with his work on the Houma Tunnel: Senator Russell Long, chairman of the Senate Finance Committee, and Hale Boggs, House Majority Whip. Victor, on friendly, first-name terms with both of them, considered them his allies.

Victor was initially wounded by the sound and tone of the investigation. It was, in fact, no more than a search, an investigation that ultimately came to the conclusion that nothing was wrong. However, that was not the way the public saw the stories. Many people confuse the term "grand-jury investigation" with something it is not, associating guilt with those who are under scrutiny.

Yet throughout all of the investigation, no one was charged with a crime connected to the House of Representatives' garage project. No one was found guilty. There was never a trial. But a pile of damaging information was leaked, and a man's reputation, built over many years, was irreparably damaged.

Many headlines savaged Victor. On 22 June 1970 *The News American* covered its front page with: "Frenkil, 8 Others Named In Secret Grand Jury Report". That same day, *The Evening Sun* headed its front page with: "U.S. Judge Meeting With Lawyers On Jury Report Linked To Frenkil". Two days later, *The News American* followed with: "Beall to Press For Indictment Against Frenkil".

The Post's first-day story quoted U.S. Attorney Stephen H. Sachs of Maryland, who was directing the investigation: "I have no specific comment at all, other than to say a special grand jury in Baltimore has been inquiring into possible violations of federal bribery laws since early this year".

The story did not indicate that, within the past five years, Stephen Sachs, the man running the investigation, had been an attorney employed by Victor's law firm, Tydings &

Rosenberg, who had represented Baltimore Contractors for more than three decades. Nowhere did newspaper articles say that, in December of 1964, Steve Sachs had represented Victor before the city's Board of School Commissioners and helped win Baltimore Contractors a contract for the $13.4 million Polytechnic-Western complex. Victor had an intense personal reaction to this situation,

From *The Evening Sun, 19 June 1970,* in the midst of the *Rayburn Parking Garage scandal.*

that he was now being investigated by someone who had recently been his legal representative. Rightly or wrongly, Victor viewed the investigation as a vindictive personal attack by Sachs, a once-trusted legal advisor who could (so Victor imagined) have had access to his books and finances. More important, it was an investigation by a confidante, one who had been paid fees by Victor's company through his law firm for 600 hours of billable time.

Nearly 35 years after the events in question, Stephen Sachs gave his account of the situation and his feelings: "The insinuation that because I had been one of Frenkil's lawyers there was something improper about my leading an investigation that focused on allegations of his wrongdoing is quite unfair.

"So long as the past representations were wholly unrelated to the new investigation — which they were — and confidences, if any, that I might have acquired in my occasional representations of Baltimore Contractors were unrelated to the new investigation — if there were any such confidences they were surely unrelated — there was no basis for my recusal," Mr. Sachs said.

Stephen Sachs recalled that, until six months before he was appointed the US Attorney for Maryland, he was an associate at Tydings & Rosenberg, which had represented Victor Frenkil and Baltimore Contractors "in many matters over the years".

He said that the firm's founder, Morris "Moose" Rosenberg, "went back a long way with VF," adding that "I was assigned to various matters, including the Poly matter....It would not surprise me that I put in 600 hours on Baltimore Contractors matters over three years. But it was the law firm, not I, that was paid many fees. I was a salaried employee. At no time, in any way shape or form, did I or, to my knowledge, Tydings & Rosenberg, have anything to do with the Underground Garage project. Whatever books and records of Baltimore Contractors I was privy to related only to the projects on which I worked and bore no relation, then or later, to the Underground Garage project. When the possibility of an investigation of Frenkil and Baltimore Contractors arose, I immediately disclosed my prior legal contacts with them to Henry Petersen, who was then the chief career lawyer in the Department of Justice's Criminal Division. He saw no problem with my continuing to lead the investigation. This approval may have been the subject of a written memo to the file."

Writing in 2004, Mr. Sachs said, "I can't dispute that VF saw the investigation as a 'vindictive personal attack'. All I can say is that I was not vindictive and had nothing to be vindictive about. The investigation stemmed from allegations received in the US Attorney's Office."

Victor, who was often suspicious of others' motivations, was now on the defensive. "My father became paranoid, and he had good reason," said Victor Jr.

Victor, who normally had sources and suppliers of information in all camps, was at a loss. For example, he was friendly with and had financially backed Maryland's Attorney General, Thomas Finan, who regularly gave him pieces of information about state business that might be useful. But, in 1969, Victor was up against a federal investigation and a hungry, ambitious federal attorney. And when Victor felt he was not in charge, he became a different person. Convinced his phones were tapped by federal agents, he started using pay phones. Friends recalled this aberration from his normal practice of tying up phone lines with multiple calls. At the same time, he never retreated from public view. In fact, he actually increased his exposure at public restaurants and gathering spots.

"My father would call me up and say, 'Let's meet at the Center Club today. I need to shake a few hands,'" recalled Victor Jr.

"He was now in a frenzy of activity. He would seem calm, rational, folding dollar bills, looking up with one eye — casting what many would regard as a manipulative countenance. He was never satisfied that he had called enough people, touched enough bases, called in enough of his chits," said Matt DeVito.

"I believe that Victor honestly felt the world was against him most of the time. He would see shadows that were not there. He would say in this regard, when I challenged him, 'You don't know,' " Matt DeVito said.

It was a bad time for the man whose trust in people was often linked with the web of obligations he had knitted. "In this connection, I don't think he had many real friends. He had Jimmy Swartz. He had few other friends. But I think others resisted entrapment. I really thought the world of Victor, and stuck by him, but I would always pick up the check when we were eating together. It was a square relationship. I didn't want the obligation to be one of 'his people'. I liked him too much personally to get that wrapped up," DeVito said.

Though Victor could not see it, the world he had thrived in was changing. Deals were not done on the basis of a handshake any more. Influential personalities were being replaced by university educators and corporate boards. The public, too, was growing more aware of, and less willing to accept, backroom deals.

"The hot water was the culmination of a style of business that was over. The world and life had changed by then. He was no longer able to do what he had done for so long," said Matt DeVito. "He had to win all this stuff [contracts] on merit. His whole capability diminished. In a few years we'd get Watergate and the whole milieu would disappear. In fact, it was going away at the time he got into hot water."

Victor was not averse to hiring lawyers. In fact, at times he engaged so many they didn't all know they were working together — or against each other. Taking their advice to heart was another matter. Matt DeVito likes to tell the story about the day he was temporarily sidelined by an acute medical problem with his stomach. He was in the hospital, flat on a table. Victor, who couldn't get him on the phone, went to the emergency room and started talking. He told DeVito that the FBI had been implying he bribed his close political buddy, Senator Daniel Brewster.

"That day I got Victor to hire Jack Jones, the most brilliant lawyer I knew," DeVito said.

Victor, sensing the danger he was in, hired extremely competent attorneys, both in Baltimore and in Washington. Many evenings, after the workday was over, his South Central Avenue office became a bullpen for legal strategies. These sessions included, among others, Jack Jones, Matt DeVito (who often sat in on them), Paul Walter, all from Baltimore, and Paul Connolly, a

Jury Report Charges Frenkil And Implicates Congressional Figures

Baltimorean Named Sole Defendant In Hushed-Up Findings

By THEODORE W. HENDRICKS

A federal grand jury report which is being kept secret by court order accuses Victor Frenkil, chief executive of Baltimore Contractors, Inc., of paying off a number of congressmen and of using threats and promises to government employees in his efforts to obtain approval of $5 million in "extras" on a federal construction job.

According to the charges, the money was paid to Senator Russell B. Long (D., La.), former Senator Daniel B. Brewster of Maryland and others.

The jury also has recommended further investigation of reports that Representative Hale Boggs (D., La.) was rewarded for his efforts on Mr. Frenkil's behalf by having work done on his home by Baltimore Contractors.

Frenkil Indictment Urged

The only person whom the grand jury recommends be indicted is Mr. Frenkil. The congressmen are named as key figures in the alleged conspiracy, although it is not recommended that they be charged. Among those named are Representative John W. McCormack (D., Mass.), the House speaker, and Nathan Voloshen, a lobbyist closely connected with Mr. McCormack who pleaded guilty last week to other conspiracy charges in New York.

DANIEL B. BREWSTER   VICTOR FRENKIL

SENATOR LONG   REPRESENTATIVE BOGGS

A report from The Sun during the investigation when the case turned to focus entirely on Victor and Baltimore Contractors.

Washington attorney from the prestigious firm of Connolly and Williams, and a Washington newcomer, William Hundley, a District of Columbia attorney with years of experience working in the Justice Department as the head of organized crime under Robert Kennedy. It proved to be an impressive, bright defense team.

Another legal advisor, attorney George McManus, who was one of Victor's longtime confidantes, recalled the "brilliant" strategy Paul Connolly employed in Victor's defense. "He was one of the brightest legal minds around at the time," Mr. McManus said.

The lawyers knew they could not stop the federal investigation. What they could do, however, was to see that the investigation never brought an indictment, which of course would bring a trial, more publicity, and, if things went really badly, a prison sentence.

"William Hundley's job was to stop the indictment," said Jack Jones. "It's always easier to avoid an indictment than to fight one."

Hundley recalls the case well. He said that Victor became his first big client after leaving the Justice Department to open a private practice.

"They could not prove what they wanted to against Victor," he said. "The only thing they had on Victor was that he had done some work on Boggs' house. That wasn't much and they knew it. It is true that Victor was aggressive. But his style wasn't that different from other contractors. They all bid low to get the job then go after the claims."

Hundley explained that what made this case different was its link to two prominent members of Congress, two men who themselves carried weight within Washington. They were big, influential targets on the hit list of an ambitious Maryland federal attorney.

"The case had really high visibility because of its connections to Senator Long and Congressman Boggs," William Hundley said. He soon learned that the Justice Department staff attorneys had decided not to indict Long or Boggs.

(There can be much legal/political theorizing about this point of the story. Paul Walter feels the senator and congressman, although both Democrats, were Southern Democrats, and thus allies to then-President Nixon. If nothing else, the two members of Congress would have known the president from his many years in Washington.)

What happened was that Justice Department staff attorneys wanted to indict Victor alone, without the trial that would attempt to take down the congressmen.

William Hundley, who at that point had never met Attorney General John Mitchell, got him to review the case.

"I didn't think it was fair, and told them so. I said, 'Look at it this way, We'll give Long and Boggs a pass, but we'll indict the Jewish contractor. Give the two pols a pass, but throw the Jewish contractor to the wolves,'" William Hundley recalled.

After a series of meetings, Attorney General Mitchell submitted the matter to his professional staff to see what ought to be done. He left it to them to see if they thought that Victor alone should be indicted.

Hundley added, "When I convinced Mitchell to review the case, he handed it to Henry Petersen, whom I had known well. We were as close as two people could be. Henry was a straight arrow. Henry had his people review it. And the people who reviewed it for Henry all concluded there would be no indictment. They didn't have a case."

In fact, the official Justice Department memorandum, dated June 12, 1970, said: "After careful review of the evidence...the staff of the Criminal Justice Division believes there is insufficient legal basis and supporting evidence to prove the charges made by the Grand Jury in this matter".

The memo named Victor Frenkil, his vice-president Bernard Shepard, their attorney Nathan Voloshen and

Senators Russell Long and Daniel Brewster and Congressman Hale Boggs.

"To fall within the statute, the conspiracy must be directed at unlawful ends and/or utilize unlawful means. The evidence elicited by the investigation of this matter does not indicate that there was any conspiracy undertaken for unlawful purposes.

"While the representatives of the Architect of the Capitol's office disagree with Frenkil and Baltimore Contractors as to the merits of the claims in this controversy, they do not doubt that he honestly believed his claims were meritorious and that the claims may in fact have some merit."

The Justice Department memo said there was "insufficient evidence" that the alleged conspirators violated the statute.

"While the conduct of Frenkil and his associates may be considered by some to have been heavy-handed, taken as a whole and viewed in the context of the substantive controversy between the Architect of the Capitol and Baltimore Contractors, Inc., neither Frenkil's conduct nor that of his other associates can be proven to be a violation of any criminal statute. Moreover, the evidence developed by the grand jury is insufficient to show any instance of corruption on the part of any Federal officers or employees of any branch of the Government."

Based on this memo, Attorney General John Mitchell declined to sign the indictment from the Baltimore Federal Grand Jury. There could be no trial against Victor Frenkil.

Stephen Sachs, who headed the investigation that brought the charges against Victor, gave this account: "I can't speak to all of Bill Hundley's dealings with the Department of Justice. Here is what I recall of mine: I dealt with Petersen, Will Wilson, chief of the Criminal Division, and Attorney General John Mitchell.

"It became obvious that the Department of Justice would not approve an indictment charging Louisiana Senator Russell Long with a crime.

"I distinctly remember John Mitchell reminding me with a wry smile that Long was chairman of the Senate Finance Committee and that it would take a far stronger case against Long to fracture the Administration's relations with that important body. I remember reluctantly acquiescing in that 'judgment call'. But I also remember pressing, by memo and in person, for an indictment of at least Frenkil and others at Baltimore Contractors. In such an indictment, of course, Long and Boggs would have to be mentioned in order to tell the story fully and accurately. I don't recall whether we proposed

The Evening Sun ran another cartoon on 24 June 1970 showing Attorney General John Mitchell, who ruled against indicting Victor, "burying" the case.

naming the elected officials as 'unindicted co-conspirators' or not, but it wouldn't have mattered. Attorney General Mitchell made it clear that he was not about to approve naming these guys. I wrote several memos protesting this decision. At one point I wrote something like 'Victor Frenkil is becoming the third-party beneficiary of a double standard erected to protect politicians'.

"I recall sitting in Mitchell's office, my memos on his desk, and his telling me in his avuncular way, puffing his pipe, that he could tell I felt 'rather strongly about this matter'.

"Bill Hundley apparently feels that his argument about 'throwing the Jewish contractor to the wolves' but giving the 'pols' a pass helped carry the day for Frenkil. I have always seen it differently: John Mitchell was not going to allow an indictment that embarrassed, even if it did not charge, important members of Congress," Mr. Sachs wrote in 2004.

What happened next was an amazing piece of legal maneuvering. While Washington had said "No" to the indictment, Baltimore was another issue. Could Stephen Sachs find a way to make his point?

"I was forbidden to sign an indictment, an instruction given me, pleasantly but precisely, by my friend Henry Petersen. I could not disobey," Mr. Sachs said in 2004. "Conscience has its claims but, as the prosecutor of the Catonsville Nine, I could hardly avoid playing by the rules. On the other hand, I was scheduled to leave office by the end of May (this was middle May as I recall) and was determined to leave a record, even if sealed, of what the evidence showed, what we recommended and what the grand jury desired.

"And so we (my principal assistant in this matter was Alan I. Baron, later my partner in private practice) told the grand jury that it was entitled to issue, under seal, a 'presentment' (an unsigned indictment), explaining that it wished to bring the charges, that the US Attorney had been forbidden to sign them and seek advice from the Court."

Victor's attorneys got wind that Stephen Sachs would try this other route, to release the contents of the grand jury report (it had been sealed, and was therefore not public information). If opened in a courtroom, it would be fair game to the press, who would then print its contents. The bad publicity would damage Victor even further. The grand jury report came under the responsibility of a Baltimore federal judge, Roszel Thompson, a member of the bench whom Victor's lawyers felt might present a problem. They knew he was friendly with Stephen Sachs. And while Victor had carefully cultivated friendships with many judges at the city, state and federal levels, they knew Roszel Thompson was not one of them. In fact, in their own level of legal paranoia, they feared he might have it in for Victor Frenkil.

"It's just known that there are judges who are predisposed to the federal side of a case. We call them 'house judges'. As a judge, Roszel Thompson was considered one of them. We were not happy with him. He was considered to be a premier house judge," William Hundley said.

In fact, Sachs wanted the grand jury's finding to be publicized. Victor's legal team thought Judge Roszel Thompson would be inclined to open the document.

The strategy was the same as before. Go to a higher authority. In this case, Roszel Thompson's superior was in Richmond, VA, home of the Fourth Federal Circuit.

Jack Jones said, "I wanted a writ of prohibition, which hadn't been issued in years. It was unusual. So one night Paul Connolly and I drove to Richmond, to the Fourth Circuit and found Judge Brand at his home. I said to him, 'You might be reluctant to sign this.' He said, 'I'm not reluctant. Give me a pen'. And it was done."

The next day the lawyers handed the writ of prohibition to Judge Roszel Thompson, who did not like being silenced by his superiors. He took it as a personal affront, and he wasn't about to be gagged. He chose to release a boiled-down synopsis, naming Victor and a staff member. It was front-page news in Baltimore.

Victor's private correspondence reveals that, by the late spring of 1970, he knew there would be no federal case against him. Word got to *The Sun's* reporter, Theodore Hendricks, who was covering the investigation for the paper. In the summer of 2003, Mr. Hendricks recalled the case. He said he doubted personally that Victor Frenkil would have ever been indicted. "He knew far too many of the federal judges and would take them to his office. I got the impression that Victor was a potent force in Baltimore. He kept a lot of people working and in jobs. That was well known and that served him well too."

As it turned out, the story of the investigation did not die a quiet death. Large portions of the original indictment made it into *The New York Times* on June 21, 1970: "Mr. Frenkil, a wealthy man and a prominent Maryland citizen who is reported to have contributed to several political campaign funds, allegedly offered people in the architect's office jobs. According to the investigation, he kept telling one of the employees that if the claims were paid, he would succeed Mr. Stewart as Capitol Architect.

"Mr. Frenkil is reported to have told one lawyer on the architect's staff that he could use a lawyer to handle Baltimore Contractors' West Virginia division at a salary in the high $20,000 range. It was also claimed that Victor offered Senator

Russell B. Long and Daniel B. Brewster $125,000 bribes, although there was never any evidence they had received any money.

"The Federal investigation also discovered that Mr. Frenkil had threatened some of the architect's employees. He allegedly told them that he would have them dismissed if the claims were not paid," *The Times* reported.

Mr. Sachs recalls leaving office at the end of May during the publicity. "Shortly thereafter *The New York Times* spread the whole story, including intimate details from the proposed indictment on the front page of its Sunday edition. I know there are those who believe that I am responsible for that leak. That is not so. I had nothing whatever, directly or indirectly, to do with it. I also had nothing whatever to do with the publicity that appeared in *The Washington Post* around Labor Day 1969."

Says Victor Frenkil Jr, "Many of the individuals involved in this scandal, including some very close to Mr. Sachs, believed he was the leak. From what I know, I believe he was".

Victor, always a fighter, was tempted to take on the press. He called his son's friend, Tony Weir, who was then working at Ogilvy & Mather in New York, to ask him to prepare a press release in response to an article in *The News American* that linked him to the Voloshen affair, part of the same investigation. Weir thought about it and sent a letter to Victor, offering advice. The letter, dated 28 October 1969, reads:

"Dear Vic:

"During our telephone conversation early this morning you told me several things:

"1. That *The News American* of October 25 had blasted you with a three-inch headline linking you to the Voloshen affair.

"2. That the publisher was so embarrassed by the coverage

(due, as I remember, to a new reporter) that he was willing to print a retraction of your choosing.

"3. That I should prepare a press release outlining the inaccuracies of *The News American* story.

"I have thought long and hard about this all day. I've reviewed the press releases I have, and I've studied the advance issue of *Life* in which your name is mentioned.

"Here, in brief summation, is what I think:

"1. You must continue to ignore the press. No matter what you say or do, no matter what you can prove, you will emerge the villain.

"2. If you do get a 'retraction' printed, you will be accused of buying out the publisher (as Mr. Levine said).

"3. Your retraction statement will not be front-page, three-inch headline news.

"4. All the so-called facts are not out yet. It is highly conceivable that anything you say in print will be used against you later. Let's assume you had made a major statement some weeks ago about this whole deal. Let's assume you had said something along the lines of, 'Mr. Sachs is crazy. All I've tried to do is the job for which I had originally been contracted. My dealings have been open and honorable'.

"5. I'd like to be the reporter who picked up the Voloshen story. I'd write a four-inch headline something like"

**"Vic Frenkil's 'open and honorable' dealings
linked to Voloshen payoff"**

"I ask you to consider a bit of Weir philosophy, a point of view I have evolved over the years. Simply stated, it goes as follows:

"1. In the curious world of public opinion, there is no such thing as *truth*.

"2. Truth, to the general public, is what the *public believes*

140

to be true.

"3. The public always believes what it *wants* to believe. And it is much more interesting to believe that a long-standing back-room kingmaker such as you is guilty than it is to believe that a man like Mr. Sachs has overstepped the bounds of credibility or decency.

"In my opinion, you can only do yourself inordinate harm by trying to answer the accusations now. They are already old news, provided somebody doesn't turn up new information. Your fighting in print will only dredge up the garbage we all want to see dumped into the ocean.

"You must be champing at the bit, anxious to attack. But I cannot see anything at this moment that you could gain from such a frontal assault. And I do see a lot you could lose.

"The shouting, for the moment, is over. The public is going back to sleep. Please don't make noise."

There was no trial. The hot water cooled and Baltimore Contractors continued doing business. Ironically, it soon had a job to build the FBI's training camp in Virginia and the company was back at work on Capitol Hill, working on a luxurious Senate office building within a decade.

Victor's emerging from the investigation relatively intact made him the talk of his political buddies. It also made a name for William Hundley, his Washington attorney, whose services were much in demand from Maryland politicians who would come under investigation during what was to be called the Watergate years. In fact, William Hundley went on to represent John Mitchell himself during the Watergate hearings. Years later, William Hundley smiled when he recalled that Victor Frenkil's case brought him considerable exposure and that, in the 1970s, he defended several other Maryland political figures brought up on charges.

Victor's case drew considerable press and editorial criticism. A lengthy article appeared in July of 1970 by nationally syndicated columnist Nicholas von Hoffman which lambasted John Mitchell's decision.

Von Hoffman said, "Mr. Frenkil is an expert at folding money. He can take a dollar bill or even a bill of higher denomination and fold it into the initials of any politician you care to name....Mr. Frenkil runs a construction company which built the parking garage in connection with the Rayburn House office building, that $10-million symbol of probity and self-denial....Indeed, it was just this pressing search for a day's pay in his days of work that attracted the attention of a grand jury, which spent 11 months looking into the matter."

Victor never gave up on the Rayburn garage issue. He kept his lawyers busy well into the 1970s. Finally, in October 1974, a federal review board rejected all but a $3,000 of a total $3.8 million cost overrun claim sought by Victor.

It may have been a Pyrrhic victory, but a victory it was.

IX. The Workaholic As Father

"If we wanted to see Dad, we called his office, made an appointment, then went to the office. After all, that's where he spent most of his time, so it made sense to us."

Victor Frenkil, Jr.

Most working parents do their best to separate their office lives from their personal lives. How many times have we all heard, "When I go home, I leave my work problems at work"? Victor Frenkil was the opposite. He had only one life — his business. Everything else, including his wife and his children, had to conform to that life.

If Victor felt the obligation to teach his children about life, then his construction company became the classroom in which the lessons were taught.

It is unlikely that he ever perceived his business as competing with his duties as a parent. Baltimore Contractors was his primary focus, so it was only natural that he should see his family as part of his business.

"If we wanted to see Dad," said Victor Jr., "we called his office, made an appointment, then went to the office. After all, that's where he spent most of his time, so it made sense to us.

"The only time we saw him for more than a few moments at home was at dinner on Sunday night. That rarely varied, unlike the other nights in the week — probably because his pals were not available for business dinners that day.

"He would often be expected home for the evening meal, then would call and say he had to take some friends to the Hibernian dinner. He worked 28 hours a day. I'm sure that, if he thought he could have gotten away with it, he would have maintained an apartment on top of his office downtown so that he could work even longer hours."

In fact, Victor had a private area next to his office with a large bathroom, a dressing room and a closet where he kept clothing so that he could go from a day's work to whatever function was awaiting him, from a crab feast at Obrycki's to a black-tie affair at the Belvedere.

In a sense, he wanted his children to be apprentices who would sit at his feet and learn from him so they could absorb his drive and determination. Their hours were his hours, their ways were his. All this made for an exhausting version of parental love.

On occasion, Victor would organize a family meeting patterned after the principles of office management. "Mom was the secretary," Victor Jr. recalled. "Dad would ask what the family needed. You were free to speak. I recommended we buy a television set. There was some discussion about the validity of the idea and, finally, he would make a decision, almost as if he were deciding whether to bid on a new job."

Janet Frenkil Krieger, the first-born child, said, "My father cared about the idea of family. He wanted more for his family than he did for himself. His siblings — Sophie, James, Bernard, Ida and Celia — were important to him. They spoke on the phone frequently. He cared that we should have a

Victor (standing second from left) and siblings around 1940.

strong relationship with his family, his brothers and sisters".

There was another time in the day when Victor spent some time with his children. Each morning, while being driven to his office, he would deposit his two sons and two daughters at their schools. "He liked to sing and we'd teach him the popular songs of the day. He really enjoyed music and he liked to hear the popular music we liked. He would often ask each of us, 'So what is your good deed for the day?' He never let up on this and we had to answer," Janet said.

While devoted to and immersed in his business, Victor was nevertheless a good domestic provider for his wife and children. When he was just 24 years old, he purchased a substantial house with apartments at 5803 Park Heights Avenue in Northwest Baltimore, which would become the family's home for a decade and the place where all four children would spend their formative years. They lived on the third floor for several years in a part of the house that was little more than an improved attic. After Victor Jr. was born, the second-floor tenant moved out and the family took over that floor, too.

Janet recalls the neighborhood as being green and suburban, with a streetcar linking it to downtown Baltimore. Although the neighborhood was then about 25 years old, there were still many vacant lots where families grew vegetables and flowers. The young Frenkil family lived on the upper floors of the house so Victor could rent the lower apartment (to a man named Gomprecht who maintained one of the adjacent gardens). One of the house rules was that the Frenkil children had to be quiet lest they bother the tenants.

Leonard Frenkil, the younger of the two sons, has a recollection of milk being delivered to the house by horse and wagon. He also remembers taking a penny he might have had in his pocket and walking to Doebereiner's Bakery to buy some three-day-old rolls.

The family's next move was to Wilton, a 32-acre estate on Reisterstown Road in Garrison, near Owings Mills, a site known today as the location of the Sweetheart Cup plant. Victor signed the purchase contract in April 1943, when he was only 34 years old, a bold move for a young father with a promising business. The splendid setting proved both a solid investment and a good place to raise a family. Some years later Victor Jr. farmed the place. He kept about ten acres under cultivation, kept pigs and two horses and milked a pair of cows each morning before leaving for school.

"Wilton was remote and I was oblivious to the world around me. We were living out in Owings Mills, with a pool, horses and a barn," Leonard Frenkil said.

Daughter Janet observed that "Victor loved the trappings that working hard provided, but I don't know about how passionate he was about providing for the family".

Wilton's rolling lawns provided a beautiful setting for Janet's wedding to Ensign Karl Frederick Krieger on 11 July 1954. The wedding reception was held outdoors amid the magnificent gardens.

Victor's dyslexia and impatience to go to work may have cut short his own college career, but he was determined that his children would not follow his example. His eldest daughter, Janet, earned a degree at Vassar College. Bebe studied engineering at Cornell. Leonard went to Johns Hopkins. Victor Jr. was something of the family rebel, who declined to enroll at college but who, like his father, turned out to be the most successful business person of all the siblings.

Daughter Janet with some guests, helping host a picnic thrown by her parents at Wilton. She would later be married at the family estate.

Like his father, he was happier and more comfortable working and getting things accomplished in the practical sense instead of theorizing about something in school. Also like his father, he had never been a good student.

Shortly before buying Wilton, Victor paid $3,000 for a summer house overlooking the Magothy River in Anne

Arundel County outside Baltimore, directly across from posh Gibson Island (the taxes were $6 a year). The place had no electricity. There was a screened porch, wooden floors partially covered in worn linoleum and an old-fashioned icebox. Water came from a well and was pumped into a holding tank. There was no radio, and the children did not learn that World War II had ended until Margaret returned from Baltimore with a newspaper that carried the story (she had been with Victor who had been operated on for appendicitis).

The house, though primitive, was popular. It became a summertime gathering place for the extended Frenkil family and was filled with cousins and friends from the end of school to Labor Day.

At one point, when the two boys were approaching their teens, Victor decided that both needed a little more polish to their speech and grammar and thought that some exposure to some well-educated friends of the same age might provide the influence they needed.

Vic discussed this with David J. Laupheimer, a friend who had been a professor of Latin and who recently had founded the Congressional Page School in Washington. Laupheimer thought for a minute and said he knew just the family, then living in Langhorne, Pennsylvania. He had taught an unusually gifted student Latin at Brown Preparatory in Philadelphia whose name was Walter Weir, then a prominent advertising executive who had two sons about the ages of Victor Jr. and Leonard.

In the late 1940s, in time for a summer vacation at the Frenkil house on the Magothy River, Victor imported Kit and Tony Weir (one of the authors of this book). Their task, though they didn't know it at the time, was to bring an element of better speech and decorum to the two Frenkil boys.

148

The Weir boys fit nicely into the Frenkil household, but the results were not necessarily those expected.

"Instead of my imparting better grammar and cultured language to Bruz (Victor Jr.), I went home at the end of the summer speaking as he did," Tony Weir recalled nearly 55 years later. "We spent most of our time talking about sex while we smoked cigarettes we had stolen, down on a little hill overlooking the water that we named 'Smoky Mountain'".

Tony and Victor Jr. have remained best friends ever since.

"The Magothy house was important to the children. I'm not so sure it was important to Dad," Janet said, "except as a place to throw big parties. It was not a chore to attend them. They were fun. Victor invited friends, political associates, children. There were always children around."

"Dad would sail down from Baltimore on a Saturday or Sunday with several friends, usually in the Rambler, a 42-foot yacht that belonged to Baltimore Contractors. He'd have dinner and sail off into the night," said Victor Jr. "Once he flew in on a seaplane, made a landing, taxied up to the shore and took everybody for a ride."

In time, Victor gave the Magothy house to his daughter Janet. Victor Jr. bought the summer house next door, which he later tore down to construct a year-round residence.

As a father, Victor believed in making all his children work. He was concerned that his own personal prosperity might allow them to become spoiled and unproductive.

As the children grew, Victor put them to work. "He was scared to death of spoiling his children," Victor Jr. said. "He was constantly repeating to us that he wanted all his children to learn the value of a dollar. We would help our mother, maybe make beds and then we'd get 15 cents. We would shine shoes or park cars when he had a party. He wanted us to

The "Rambler", the company yacht that, on sunny Friday afternoons, often took Vic and guests to his summer cottage on the Magothy River.

understand the value of a dollar. He worked our asses off.

"Dad believed strongly in saving what you made (something he preached more than practiced). He always said, 'Whatever you save, I'll match for you in a bank account so you can buy a car.' You might even say that he invented the 401(k) program."

"We were all required to work," his son Leonard said. "But as the child of a wealthy father, there could be some unusual consequences. One summer my father got me a job at Locke Insulator in South Baltimore. The work was demanding.

"At 4:30 in the morning our chauffeur would awaken me to drive me to work by 6. I recall one day sitting around having lunch. It must have been a Friday because my mother entertained on Thursdays. There I was at Locke insulator with all these guys and I was eating stuffed squab, because that was what we had in the house," Leonard Frenkil said.

"He wanted everyone to have a job. Dad was the recruiter.

He had a slot for everyone in the family, his sons, daughters, grandchildren and in-laws. I was picked to run Baltimore Contractors and was assigned to the Houma Tunnel job in Louisiana. Maybe it was a Jewish thing, with my father being the patriarch of the family," Victor Jr. said. "When working with Victor it was not easy. He dominated. You could not even pick out the color of paint in the boiler room."

Victor wanted his second child, Vida, to follow him in construction. Indeed, at Forest Park High School, her favorite subjects were science and math. She was the only female in shop class. She studied civil engineering at Cornell University and went to work on several important Baltimore Contractors projects, including the Bel Air High School and the Civic Center in downtown Baltimore. She also had artistic skills and painted the portrait of John Eager Howard that hangs in the Belvedere Hotel above a fireplace in a room named for the Revolutionary War general. She also ran the Belvedere Hotel renovation project when her father owned the hotel.

Typical of the way Victor wanted his family to behave was the situation in September 1961, while son Victor Jr. was laboring in the heat of a late Louisiana summer. That month, his 27-year-old daughter Vida, who then had two children, was in downtown Baltimore working on another pet project, the construction of the Civic Center. Victor must have beamed at the flattering newspaper story and picture that appeared in *The Sun* under the heading "Mother Helps Make Civic Center". The construction, she said, was "more interesting than housework. And besides, it pays better". She was the only woman on the $8-million construction job and handled all the paper work for Baltimore Contractors. She was described as dodging piles of structural steel "in sensible, low-heeled shoes, dusty slacks and the required safety helmet".

Mother Helps Make Civic Center

Matron On Construction Project Says Her Job "Pays Better" Than Housekeeping

By FRANK P. L. SOMERVILLE

Building a Civic Center may not be every young matron's cup of tea, but Vida Davis thinks it's "more interesting than housework."

"And besides, it pays better," she adds with a ready smile.

The only woman on the nearly $8,000,000 construction job, she handles all its paper work for Baltimore Contractors, Inc.

Manages The Office

She is the downtown project's office manager, cost accountant and timekeeper, among other things.

Sidewalk superintendents peering from the fringes of the big building site at Hopkins place and Baltimore street have been doing double-takes with good reason.

Mrs. Davis, at 27, is what the fashion magazines would call petite even when, clipboard in hand, she is dodging piles of structural steel in sensible, low-heeled shoes, dusty slacks and the required safety helmet.

She has an almost proprietary interest in the Civic Center and shows not a little impatience with the public controversy and municipal turmoil that keep intruding on the project.

At Ease With 'Taxpayers'

"Let's look at the good side—what a wonderful building it's going to be," she enthuses brightly.

Mrs. Davis proves to be equally at ease with brawny ironworkers and "the taxpayers" (as she labels all inquisitive passersby), and it comes as no surprise that she once handled public relations for Baltimore Contractors.

She is working her way through all departments of the company.

Although her current job is her first in accounting, she has held other responsible positions on a number of large building projects.

Her formal training included two years of civil engineering courses at Cornell.

At Forest Park High School, where she was a student less than a decade ago, Mrs. Davis was the only girl in the "shop" course and revealed an unusual talent for fixing radios.

"Science and math were always my favorite subjects," she explains.

The mother of two young chil(Continued, Page 19, Column 1)

MRS. VIDA DAVIS
The Civic Center's only chic construction worker

Daughter Vida, known as "Bebe", studied civil engineering at Cornell and, for a while, worked for Victor on a variety of construction jobs. An independent person, she was the only woman on the Civic Center job in 1961.

"Mrs. Davis (Vida) starts her bustling work day at 7 o'clock every morning and doesn't put down her clipboard and turn her red sports car homeward until 4:15 or later," the 1961 newspaper article noted.

Despite Victor's competitive spirit and ruthlessness in his business dealings, he had a curious side: He could not fire an employee. He did not like bumping heads with the people he directly dealt with. Family members said he had the muscle and he had the finesse, but he could not end a relationship. When it was painfully obvious that someone had to go, he would bring in another person, a friend, to do the dirty work.

Friends of Victor often noted he did not waste time and emotion in cultivating true, intimate friendships. While he may have been a friend, or what was really an acquaintance, of hundreds of people, more often these were business relationships based upon sales or gaining an advantage. Given his Jewishness, and how he felt it affected his career, he was a natural loner, a thoroughly private person.

The one person in his life that Victor did trust was Jimmy Swartz. Indeed, as their fathers before them had been friends, Victor was an intimate of James M. Swartz, a furrier and real estate investor well known in Baltimore who was about ten years senior to Victor.

Victor often took his problems to Swartz, an ex-Marine and World War I veteran who was tough and capable of making hard decisions. Swartz also hobnobbed with politicians and was no doubt a mentor to Victor. Swartz was a lifelong friend of Dr. H. C. "Curley" Byrd, president of the University of Maryland at College Park. Through Dr. Byrd, Swartz met and visited President Dwight D. Eisenhower at his Gettysburg, Pennsylvania farm. He also knew President Harry S. Truman and British Prime Minister Winston Churchill. Victor delighted in this sort of exposure and access to personages whose names filled the news media. The two friends called each other frequently and compared notes on politicians they had an interest in pursuing.

"Jimmy and my father were so entangled in politics they had secrets the world would love to know. They were the best of friends," Victor Jr. said.

Jimmy also functioned smoothly within the Frenkil family. In 1958, when Margaret and Victor were attending the Brussels World's Fair, Victor Jr. decided to marry, even though his parents were away. Jimmy Swartz gave him money for a ring, after which he and his sweetheart Nancy ran off and got married.

In the early 1960s, Victor Jr. gave working for his father his best effort. He soon found the role impossible. "My father was always giving advice. He would say, 'There's always a better way, let me show you.' It was his way, of course. He was never satisfied. He always wanted to build that better mousetrap. Yet he was brilliant. He could out-think, out-maneuver, out-work and out-meddle anybody. His mind never stopped working. He never gave up on anything he set out to do. He was like a dog with a bone. He didn't know how to quit."

Shortly after his marriage to Nancy, Victor Jr. accepted his father's assignment to leave Baltimore for several years and move to rural, coastal Houma, Louisiana, and supervise a major, multi-million project, a tunnel under the Intercoastal Waterway. It was tough work. As the local paper noted, he "was the first to arrive and the last to leave". The tunnel project (which in hindsight was never a project that Baltimore Contractors should have bid) was beset by troubles. It nearly undermined the newlyweds' marriage.

Once the construction side of the job was finished, Victor

Jr. was put in charge of building the Maryland Pavilion of the 1964 World's Fair in Flushing, New York. This also meant moving out of state.

"Living in New York was not so much fun. I also didn't like the union rules there," Bruz said. "The New York unions were powerful and ruled everything. It wasn't my style."

After these two experiences, Victor Jr., then 27 years old, decided to go into a business by himself, one where he could call the shots. While he was willing to remain under the umbrella of the Frenkil empire, he had to distance himself from his father.

"I loved the guy, and I respected him greatly, but by God it was difficult to work under him. He micromanaged everything. He had such tunnel vision about work that he never considered that there might be another way to do things. His way was the only way. It was suffocating."

Victor owned several businesses that were not directly under his thumb like Baltimore Contractors. One was Jarvis Lumber, in southwest Baltimore, which he bought because of the several acres of real estate that went with the business. In the mid-1960s, Victor Jr. was able to move to Jarvis to run the business, then headed by one of Victor's brothers-in-law, Abe Greenberg (who was married to Victor's sister, Ida).

Jarvis dealt in southern yellow pine and its annual sales were setting no records. Under the same roof was a salvage business, U.S. Wrecking, another of Victor's companies. (He loved the idea of making cash on the sale of old building materials. It was cash-and-carry and in pure Victor logic: Who needs a full four-by-eight piece of plywood when you can sell him scrap?)

Jarvis got into the steel business during a steel strike several years later. Baltimore Contractors on South Central Avenue was a union shop. Jarvis, in southwest Baltimore's Westport, was non-union. Victor Jr. started fabricating and selling steel, a change in the original business that eventually came to dominate the lumber sales.

Delighted with the independence, Victor Jr. decided to reach for more by buying the Jarvis operation outright from his father and relocating it to a larger site in the Brooklyn section of the city. This was difficult. Victor did not like parting with assets. He did not like surrendering control. It was bad enough to have his son out of Baltimore Contractors, which Victor always dreamed his son would someday run, but cut loose, entirely outside Victor's sphere, would be tough to swallow.

"The day I faced my father down and asked him to cut me free was one of the toughest times in my life. I used his type of logic against him by saying, 'You've never held anybody back in your life. You've always pulled people forward'. I eventually convinced him. My father told me, 'Do what you want'."

From this time on, Victor Jr. and his father remained close and devoted to one another. But their businesses were separate, which is likely to have permitted the strong relationship they maintained, largely because Victor was no longer the boss.

It fell to his younger son, Leonard, to run Baltimore Contractors after Victor's death. For many years Leonard had been an executive of the firm, watching Victor run his life and the lives of those around him.

"He was street smart. He had this primal sense that other people don't possess. He could read people. It was hard to bullshit him. When a person lies, the body puts out something, and he could detect that lie," Leonard said.

Leonard also felt his father genuinely loved people (although in an abstract sense) and, when he wanted, had incredible social skills. At such moments he was usually working to achieve some end.

"Victor was very direct, immediate, an incredibly bright man. He was often five steps ahead of you mentally. In his prime, he would take you to the brink, then know just when to back off. There would be times when he consciously could break a person. As tough as Victor could be, he had a soul and he would cave. In the end, he was really a soft touch."

Leonard also considered his father to be clairvoyant, or at least had the ability to sense impending trouble.

Leonard recalled a time when he was running one of Victor's investments, the Colmar Apartments in North Baltimore. Victor often called his son during the day, but this day, he kept questioning, "Is everything all right?"

"I felt it was funny. He called again, 15 minutes later. 'Is everything all right?' No," I said, "we have a fire."

"On another occasion, I was driving him home. He told me to turn back and go to Charles and Centre, to an old hotel that was due to be torn down for a senior-citizen apartment house. I thought he wanted to scavenge something from it, because he was an inveterate scavenger. We parked in a lot alongside. Then he told me to look upstairs to one of the upper floors. Not all the electricity in the building was turned off. I saw a light and it was moving. He said, 'Go call the fire department'."

Working with his father, Leonard soon realized that "He was a person who always needed to be in charge, openly or behind the scenes. He made a lot of enemies, but he started with a lot of enemies because he was Jewish.

"He was a wise man on important issues. He would go into a meeting with complicated presentations. He'd cut though all the dull subterfuge and come up with the real issue. He had a strong sense of what was the core issue. He could read people and situations with blazing precision," Leonard said.

"On the job site, he was keenly aware of appearance. [Ed. note: For Victor, each job site was an extension of himself, and he was extremely aware of his image, recognizing that how he was perceived would enhance — or detract from — that image.] He wanted the job site to be neat and tidy. He took great pride in his work. And if a job lost money, he'd eat you alive.

"He was ego-driven. If he had an Achilles' heal, it was that he wanted recognition for the important things he did."

In the late 1950s, Victor and Margaret sold Wilton and moved into The Marylander, the apartment house Victor had built five years earlier. Their children were now growing up or already married. Soon grandchildren would arrive and Victor and Margaret would have another generation of their own.

"He loved children. He himself was a big kid. He loved games, toys, stunts, child-like fun. Kids are pretty discerning. They liked him and his gadgets, and were drawn to his origami," said friend Matt DeVito.

"In many ways Victor was kind and generous. His best time was when he was unconnected with anything he wanted in business. He was then thoughtful and interested. I can see his driver coming up to my house with a bag of beautiful, gorgeous grapefruit as a gift. He would just leave it. That was Victor's kind and thoughtful side showing through.

"I was always impressed at how Victor was a caring husband and father. Plus Margaret was a wonderful lady," DeVito said.

"And yet, at a restaurant, he would order for me: 'you'll have the crab cake', or 'the shad roe is good', without questioning what I might want. He would also lecture me: 'Matt, stop biting your nails.'

"I was impressed that he lived simply. Had a car and driver, and that was about all. He was certainly not a flashy dresser. When he entertained, it was mostly in restaurants," DeVito reported.

DeVito recalled a charming meal that Margaret made when the three of them were together, a lunch of iceberg lettuce, hardboiled eggs, sardines in oil and sliced tomatoes, with dark Jewish rye bread on the side. It was the meal the Frenkils had been served when first married and living in a Linden Avenue rooming house. The landlady included breakfast in their rent and this was a dish she served regularly.

If there was another way that Victor played the grandfatherly patriarch, it was producing his annual Christmas card. (He may have been Jewish, but was willing to honor this holiday, probably because of Margaret and the children.)

He and Margaret, who really organized the card, assembled their children and grandchildren and outfitted everyone in red

One of the annual Christmas card photographs of the extensive Frenkil family in red seasonal garb, this one taken in front of son Victor Jr.'s barn in Reisterstown (Victor Jr. is the one holding the horse).

pajamas, nightshirts and gowns. This produced an enormous annual family portrait.

There was another place where his grandchildren could see their grandfather without bells going off: Barren Island.

"He did love playing with his grandchildren in a very restricted environment. There were no distractions. His grandchildren remember him fondly for the time spent there. He gave them all nicknames," his daughter Janet said. One of his favorite activities was "Follow the leader" (with Victor, of course, as leader). Ever nimble, he would climb over sofas, walk on the rough-hewn wooden tables, with the kids following him as if he were the Pied Piper.

While Victor seemed to enjoy Barren Island, his visits were always short. After all, he (not unlike other addicts) could not indulge himself with his favorite drug — the telephone.

Of course, Barren Island was not immune to business entertaining, and Victor did a lot of it there. It was ideal if one wanted intimate conversations with no distractions, or if one had friends who liked to hunt ducks and geese.

If one were to ask Victor today how he felt about his family, it is most likely he would express deep affection for all, and would believe that he had done his very best to help them grow into healthy, contributing human beings.

How could he think otherwise, since he had brought up his children *his* way, which was, after all, the *only* way?

X. Favorite Child

"Sweet to the father is his first-born's birth..."
George Gordon, Lord Byron

For nearly 70 years he shepherded Baltimore Contractors, his beloved firm, which was a natural extension of the human being Victor had become. Like a first-born child, he fathered it, guided it, worked diligently to make it succeed and, when it got in trouble, spent whatever was necessary to help it.

As much as Victor Frenkil sought the attention of those who held power, he did it with a purpose (there was little Victor did that was without an ulterior motive). He was always seeking work for Baltimore Contractors which, in its later years, often did more than $100 million worth of business on an annual basis.

He began by building a front porch, rising to build the largest office building in the state of Maryland. Not a conservative businessman (or man, for that matter), he relished taking risks and never said no to a job. He was so competitive that he is likely to have seen two advantages in taking a job: first, he got it and, second, a competitor didn't.

He took particular pleasure in completing jobs with acutely troubled histories and actually enjoyed the stories he could then tell on himself about the projects that blew up in his face. Like an addicted gambler, whatever money he made he put back on the table of his life's passion, the construction game he played until the day he died.

"He never slowed down," said his son, Victor Jr. "In his 80s he was still reaching, working to build his business. He was never satisfied with the unusual success he had achieved."

Victor was, of course, interested in winning. But that was not the ultimate goal. It was the playing of the game that so intrigued him.

Newspapers occasionally portrayed him as a combination of a political crony, powerful insider and a publicity hound. This indeed was one side of his demeanor. But along the way, Victor contributed substantially to his city and state. And, over the years, he directed a small army (600 persons in the 1970s) of faithful employees who doted on his fatherly, intense, and occasionally heavy-handed ways.

"He drove them and drove them again, night and day. He made them fly at night to save time that could be dedicated to work. And in spite of all this, his employees loved him — not without reason. He listened to them. Their problems were his problems. If an employee had a family hardship, he was there, usually handing them cash," recalled Victor Jr.

"One of the principal jobs of his long-time corporate secretary, Virginia Lambrow, was helping remember anniversaries and sending flowers to the widows of the men who had worked for Dad."

"You've got to take a personal interest in each individual and their families. The big shot, the little shot, the side shot, they're all the same to me," Victor said in 1976 in an interview in *The Equipment Dispatch*, an industry publication.

"I hire the man who's had many jobs rather than one job

because of the exposure he's had," he said in same article.

"His long-term employees were incredibly loyal to him. The people my father hired fell into two categories. They would come and go in a hurry or they would stay forever," said Victor Jr.

"He knew how to hold on to his employees even though he never paid tremendous salaries," said Salvatore Manfre, one of his loyal associates. "He had a knack for keeping people happy and satisfied. At the annual Christmas party, he would give out awards recognizing your years with Baltimore Contractors. This was very important to him. He would also issue shares in company stock. In a way, it was another way of passing out something without giving something away out-of-pocket. But it helped establish loyalty."

Victor, who delighted in entertaining, believed in company functions. There was an annual employees' summer outing and a Christmas party. In the days when racial segregation prohibited his African-American employees from entering the hotels where the Christmas parties were staged, Victor threw a separate party at a Masonic hall for his black employees and their guests. He also required the white company executives to join him at the separate function at which prizes and awards were also distributed.

To grasp Victor Frenkil's highly personalized way of conducting business, one needs to dig into his behavior. While his style occasionally landed him in hot water, such as the time he was pursued by federal prosecutors in 1970, his Byzantine, highly personal business ways often contributed to his gaining the large contracts he sought.

"My father loved a challenge. He liked to make a million dollars and then take on something where he'd lose a million," said Victor Jr.

"He enjoyed the battle even more than the victory," observed Tony Weir, who saw Victor as a freewheeling deal-maker. "It wasn't the construction business that intrigued him. It could have been yachts or used cars. He didn't care about the technical aspects and the details of jobs as much as he did about the quest for them, going after a project, winning it and then gaining the visibility from the win."

A contented Victor Frenkil poses for the camera at his home in 1948. Business was looking up and he felt more secure about his ability to keep it growing.

Consider a day in November 1953 when Victor and Baltimore Contractors were on a high. His company was 20 years old and he was now successful. His crew had recently completed the eastern causeway of Maryland's Chesapeake Bay Bridge, which would go down as the state's pre-eminent public works project of the century. (He would later get a good chunk of a huge water-distribution pipe under the I-95 freeway between Baltimore and the Susquehanna River, another plum that led him to boast, rightfully, that the city's drinking water flowed through his work.)

On this day, he had hired three cars of a Pennsylvania Railroad express train to Philadelphia to see the Army-Navy football game. As Victor and his staff deftly choreographed this artful public relations outing, it was no ordinary gathering.

Early on, Victor established a Baltimore Contractors public relations department headed by William Potts. Mr. Potts and his staff worked hard at their duties, which were directed at employees, clients, friends of the company and, of course, those who could lead to new business. Thanks to office records that survived, it is possible to see how minutely this day was planned to delight and impress those who were invited and accepted. In the Frenkil style, all his children were involved, and all retain their memories of it.

"That was a very special day, with the chartered train and the dining cars. People just cannot travel with that style any more," said his daughter, Janet Frenkil Krieger.

"My father never cared about getting the greatest seats in the stadium. For him, it was about getting people together. Seat locations were not important. It was about pleasing his people," said Victor Jr. "If he had an event, he'd have photographers along too, and after a few days, the guests would receive photographs of themselves with other important people at whatever party my father threw."

An office memorandum preserves the order of business: "8:30 a.m. P.R.R. Special Train BA-1 will be ready for occupancy at Penn Station, Baltimore. Next to locomotive will be a coach with entrance at the front end. Next will be two dining cars. These three cars are for our exclusive use. 9 a.m. As guests arrive, they will be assigned coach space…for the placing of wraps, and dining car space, where they will sit both going and coming."

There was a carefully preordained, strict seating plan distributed to key Baltimore Contractors employees, which was not to be made public. Very little was left to chance. Designated employees were to "take the seat at the assigned table, next to the aisle, and facing Philadelphia".

"You will act as the host for all the guests at your pair of tables, in the diner, in the coach, at the game. You will see that everyone is congenially acquainted with the others, and that each feels as though the party were really for him."

"The breakfast menu [printed on heavy stock with a heading 'Baltimore Contractors Party'] has been standardized: orange juice, hot cream of wheat with cream, broiled ham with eggs (choice of style of eggs), toast and wheat muffins with butter and marmalade, choice of coffee, tea or milk. The more elaborate steak dinner menu [for the return] has also been standardized. Please diplomatically discourage any exceptions."

The rules of the day stated "There will be no alcoholic beverages served with breakfast. Miniatures will be made available before guests leave the train at Philadelphia. The dining-car stewards have been instructed to serve alcoholic beverages at the table on the return trip, only as directed by Mr. Frenkil in one diner, and by Mr. Levine in the other.

"At the door between our second diner and the public train,

there will be a sign indicating ours is a private party. The door must not be locked, and Mr. Roche will politely turn back any would-be crashers.

"Miss Vida Frenkil will distribute the Glamor Lunch Kits and the thermos bottles of coffee along with sandwiches and cake in the diner in which she sits, and Miss Janet Frenkil will distribute these items in the other diner. Miss Lambrow will distribute tickets to the game."

And lastly: "Be entirely familiar with, and cooperative in, the timing and the plans, but lend the atmosphere of informal, easy enjoyment, as you like in your own home. You will represent the Company to your group of guests. We are all sure you will measure up to your opportunity."

Also surviving is an amazingly well connected guest list, one that in 1950s must have been the envy of his industry. Among the invitees were Frenkil favorites: Senator George L. Radcliffe; Chief Baltimore Judge Anselm Sodaro; City Council member Arthur Price; Judge Dulaney Foster; Governor Theodore McKeldin; Governor Millard Tawes; State Comptroller Louis Goldstein; Admiral Ben Moreell; radio station owner Jake Embry; University of Maryland president "Curley" Byrd; House of Representatives member George Fallon; Senator Herbert R. O'Conor; Judge Joseph Carter; Arthur Grotz, president of the Western Maryland Railway; and Robert Hobbs, president of the Maryland National Bank. And to make sure his name was never omitted from the city's principal newspaper, present were *Baltimore Sun* city editor Edwin P. Young Jr., *Sunday Sun* editor Harold Williams and the paper's star feature photographer, A. Aubrey Bodine.

"I sometimes wondered if all his courting of the politicians did him any real good," said Leonard Hudson, his long-time corporate president. "It may have helped in some places and it

may have also cost him jobs. Not everyone liked all this attention and going to dinners. Some businessmen that Victor
courted just liked to get the job done and go home at night."

"Do I think he got his money's worth? Business-wise, maybe no. But emotionally, he did. My father loved to entertain. I
think when he first started his business, and business in general was conducted on a more personal, one-to-one basis, I think
the entertaining helped him quite a bit. But the times changed
— and he did not," Victor Jr. said.

For all of Victor's extravagant entertaining, many of his jobs
came though normal business practice. Salvatore Manfre, who
worked with him for decades, estimates that 80 percent of
Victor's work was won though straight bidding on advertised
jobs. "He liked to think that he went out and got contracts in
his hip pocket through personal negotiation. But, in truth, 80

*A typical Baltimore Contractors extravaganza hosted by Victor, this one a
dinner at the Belvedere Hotel for his employees, 20 December 1947.*

percent of his work came from hard bidding. He had capable, competent people he relied upon. He was not easy on them, but he believed in them."

Mr. Manfre said he did not think that Victor could actually read a construction drawing. "He may not have been articulate, but he possessed a seventh sense about a project. He was a good judge and he had an innate comprehension of things. He could also smell a good job and reject one that he would call a 'pie in the sky.' When he came on a job site, he would see things that were not obvious to me, but were thoroughly obvious to him."

Victor, commenting on his approach to business, often said, "Do things for enough people over enough years and they may get something done for you." Then he would add with his wry smile, "But don't count on it".

Victor's office staff preserved many telling documents from the 1950s that illustrate his aggressive approach to public relations. Each Christmas, in addition to mailing a well drawn Baltimore Contractors' card showing Santa flying over the 711 South Central Avenue building, he staged a stag party for his friends and customers. Within the company, he posted rules that discouraged too much drinking or carousing. He had cabs waiting at the door should any guest imbibe too much. He also hired professional exotic dancers and striptease artists who performed in one of the company's sheds. Invitations to these parties were much coveted.

Victor could be shrewd and canny about the construction business, but he was also an inveterate risk-taker. Over the years, he had gone out on many flimsy limbs, although he always used these experiences to guide his hand on his next job. He often remarked he did not believe in luck. "Luck is what you make it," he would say.

Victor's hiring practices reflected his involvement in the business. Over the years, he hired many presidents, but never let them make important decisions. "He'd hire everybody to be president of the company but he would not let anyone run the company but himself," said Victor Jr.

As a reminder of what can go wrong on a job, Victor kept a large framed photo of the Aquia Creek Bridge in his office. The picture of a passenger train crossing the span was not mere decoration. It was an ever-present visual reminder warning

The Aquia Creek Bridge. Victor lost so much money on the job that he kept this photo hanging in his office to remind him of what not to do.

him never to be caught short or unprepared for the worst possible situation.

The project originally appealed to him because it was large and involved heavy construction, then traditionally not open to Jews.

Baltimore Contractors won the $400,000 contract in 1946 to rebuild a double-track bridge over Aquia Creek for the

Richmond, Fredericksburg and Potomac Railroad, the company that carried a considerable amount of passenger and freight traffic along the East Coast. The Virginia span was located on the main passenger rail connection south from Washington. At the time, this was an important piece of bridgework. It was also the kind of job Victor wanted to do, a piece of heavy construction whose completion would show he had made the transition from small, Baltimore-centered jobs to a larger arena. This was also the kind of job that eventually got him in trouble. If Victor Frenkil had a fault, it was taking on jobs that were out of his league, too big for his aspirations. But without those aspirations to expand Baltimore Contractors, the company would have been mediocre.

One day Victor received a call from his site manager: A subcontractor who owned and operated a floating pile driver had walked off the job. Five years later such a thing would have been a trifle, but Baltimore Contractors was young and did not have equipment at its disposal. There were severe materials and equipment shortages at the end of World War II. Some of his people told Victor to give up and declare bankruptcy. He was told there was not a floating rig left in the county to be had. He was also told that the ones left all belonged to the military.

"What branch of the military is the most likely to have one?" Victor asked. He was told the Seabees, the division of the Navy that specialized in building docks, piers and bridges in combat zones, frequently coming in on the first wave and working under enemy fire.

"Well I'll have to get it from the Seabees," Victor said. Then, according to the story, everyone at the table laughed.

Victor made inquiries and learned that the commander of the Seabees was Admiral Ben Moreell, a tough old Navy man who worked long days at his Washington office. The advance word was that Admiral Moreell would have little sympathy for a civilian who wanted to borrow his equipment to build a civilian railroad bridge in Virginia.

Victor took off for the Admiral's Washington office, was ushered in and was met by two icy eyes glowering at him behind a big desk piled with papers.

"What can I do for you, Mr. Frenkil?" the Admiral asked. He sounded like a man who had little time to waste on a civilian with political connections.

"I want you to lease me a floating rig so I can finish a bridge in Virginia. The project is critical to the area [it indeed was]. I don't need the rig for very long, but I have to have it. There is no other option."

Moreell stared at Victor. The muscles in his jaw rippled. "You've got a lot of nerve asking me for that," he said. "But, given your nerve, I guess we can accommodate you." So Victor got the rig and finished the job to the railroad's satisfaction.

"The Aquia Creek Bridge job was Dad's diploma. It was his first step into heavy construction," said Victor Jr. "His friends in the industry told him to stay away, it's a different business from what you are used to. The more he was told to stay away, the more he came back. He would take a job without knowing what it really entailed. But he'd finish it, somehow. He then came back for more. In the end, he never made any money in heavy construction. But he always enjoyed trying."

In typical Frenkil style, Victor later put Admiral Moreell on his board of directors. When the chief Seabee visited Baltimore, Victor had newspaper reporters ready to interview him. Admiral Moreell, who by all accounts was a brilliant business executive, took his duties seriously and once issued a blistering memo to Victor that Baltimore Contractors needed to be more profitable. He also lambasted Victor's habit of serving heavy lunches at his meetings, meals the admiral felt left the attendees drowsy.

Victor courted favorable publicity about Baltimore Contractors and himself. He thought that media attention gave him one of the goals he constantly sought, which he called "exposure". Exposure could mean being seen and recognized at a crowded restaurant. It also meant his face and story, favorably reported of course, in a newspaper. Of all the many articles written about Baltimore Contractors and its chief, few actually captured Victor with any perception. One, written by sports reporter Richard Kucner for the *News American* in 1968, caught some of Victor's philosophy:

"Victor Frenkil sits behind a large desk, speaking softy but intently, choosing his words carefully and releasing them with conviction and self-assurance.

"'All life is a race. Everything is on a comparative basis… everything. When you look at a picture, you subconsciously compare the shapes, colors, etc. In business and in sports, you constantly compare yourself and your ability against everyone else's. Every day, business is a gamble. You make decisions and you may win or lose by them. Eventually, the burden becomes unwieldy and you reach a point of diminishing returns if you try to do it alone. You have to bring in associates and assistants.'" The reporter noted that Victor often repeated the words "desire" and "competitive".

In classic understatement, he said in the article, "You've got to put in the hours; you've really got to spend the time." What Victor did not say would have been more revealing still: "The hours I put in may seem long and demanding to most, but to me it's a game I thoroughly enjoy. So it really isn't work!"

"It's hard to say. Maybe my father lost more than he made," said Victor Jr. "When he bid and built the Houma Tunnel, he

A pier and rock storage shed, one of the jobs Baltimore Contractors completed for the National Gypsum Company.

lost $1.25 million. It came right out of his pocket. He would never declare bankruptcy. He sold his assets instead to keep Baltimore Contractors going. He took the Marylander Apartments, which had been a great investment and a cash cow, sold the property and dumped its proceeds into his company. He would say of Baltimore Contractors, 'This is where it's been and this is where it's going to be.'"

And indeed, for the projects that Victor had to bail out, he had another collection of highly profitable winners. Oddly enough, although he used these successful projects in his publicity materials over the years, he seemed to derive a greater pleasure discussing the ones that backfired on him.

Even though he may not have called much attention to them around his friends and political cronies, Victor had long-time relationships with clients who came back to him over the years. In the 1940s he secured a contract for a U.S. Gypsum Plant and waterfront pier in the Canton section of Baltimore. His relationship with the gypsum industry was enduring (he built plants in Burlington, New Jersey, among other cities) and indeed, at the time of his death at the age of 90, he was about to begin another job.

Because of his relationship with University of Maryland president "Curley" Byrd, a close friend of Victor's brother, James, he constructed much at the school's College Park campus, including the William P. Cole Field House, Byrd Stadium, several dormitories and fraternity houses, the student union, the Glenn L. Martin Institute of Technology, as well as the men's and women's swimming pools.

His building relationships with the State of Maryland extended to the 1964 World's Fair in Flushing, New York, where he built Maryland's pavilion). About a decade later, Baltimore Contractors built what was then the largest state-owned office complex, the Herbert R. O'Conor Building in downtown Baltimore. In a joint venture with the Ralph M.

Baltimore Contractors built this restaurant for the Howard Johnson's chain on Washington Boulevard in Baltimore.

Baltimore Contractors did a lot of school construction work, this the Bel Air High School in Bel Air, Harford County, Maryland.

Parsons Company, he enlarged Baltimore-Washington International Airport. This was a $65-million contract.

For the City of Baltimore he constructed its largest high school, the Baltimore Polytechnic Institute-Western High School complex, and the Hollander Ridge Housing Project. In the early 1960s, when Baltimore was beginning to rebuild its downtown, the Baltimore Contractors sign rose over the Civic Center, where Victor's daughter Vida worked for several years. He also completed a drinking-water source for Baltimore in the early 1960s, when the Maryland portion of the I-95 Interstate Highway was being built. When another contractor could not do the job, Baltimore Contractors stepped in and built an underground viaduct that, in times of a drought, would supply water from the Susquehanna River to Baltimore's reservoirs. This $49 million spent to supply drinking water to Baltimore has eased numerous water shortages during extended hot and dry spells.

Victor, who had barely squeaked through high school, received an unusual accolade on 29 May 1961 from the Steed

College of Technology in Johnson City, Tennessee. It read:

"Victor Frenkil: In recognition of a distinguished career as engineer in the service of home improvement and industrial development in various states, for the Federal Government, and foreign countries...

"In recognition of the creation and establishment of a successful industrial construction firm, abundantly meeting the needs of the United States and many other nations in the form of underwater tunnels, dormitories, hospitals, stadiums, giant-size industrial plants, and bridges...

"In recognition of significant contributions to the field of health and education, and the creation of scholarships for deserving high school graduates, and the establishment of a free, educational program for the benefit of employees of Baltimore Contractors, Inc., who desire to continue their education...

"In recognition of outstanding leadership in the promotion of the Fine Arts and cultural institutions, richly influencing the social and spiritual life of your city of Baltimore...

"In recognition of devoted service to your city as a public-spirited citizen, and as a student of modern technological advancement in engineering, you are in close kinship with the ideals of the college...

"In recognition of these distinctions and many others, it is, therefore, my privilege to recommend to you, President Steed, Victor Frenkil, for the degree, Doctor of Engineering."

It was signed, "C. W. Doss, Dean".

Directly underneath the signature it read: "Victor Frenkil, upon recommendation of the faculty and with the approval of the Board of Directors of Steed College of Technology, by the authority vested in me by the State of Tennessee, I hereby confer upon you the degree, Doctor of Engineering, with all the rights, privileges and responsibilities thereunto appertaining."

It was signed, "C.C. Steed, President".

Not bad for a dyslexic with a dismal educational record.

Although Victor savored the exposure that constructing the Rayburn Garage and the Dirksen Senate Office Building carried, these projects were not moneymakers and, in fact, cost him. He and his staff discussed these projects constantly.

It is telling that he spoke less about his highly successful work such as constructing major additions to historic Bancroft Hall at the Naval Academy at Annapolis. Baltimore Contractors finished this job with little fanfare other than several newspaper feature stories discussing the project. It was a successful and profitable venture, like so many others that made his firm a powerful player. But because of its uneventful history, and Victor's taste for controversy and delight in beating the odds, he found little to discuss in it.

Opening of the Golden Sands in Ocean City, July 1975. From left: Mayor Harry Kelley, Victor, wife Margaret, Louis Goldstein, Francis Burch (Maryland Attorney General) and son Leonard.

In this vein, he also built the Medical Biological Laboratory for the Army Corps of Engineers at Fort Detrick in western Maryland, the Federal Bureau of Investigation's Quantico, Virginia, training complex, the Walter Reed Army Medical Center's Institute of Pathology in Silver Spring, Maryland, and an important section of an Interstate Highway known as the Air Rights Tunnel in downtown Washington. The profits realized from these helped cover the unsuccessful risks Victor so frequently accepted.

He did like to talk about two of his more exotic ventures, a racetrack in Puerto Rico (El Comandante Hipódromo) and the Lajes Field landing strip and barracks in the Azores off the coast of Spain, where he would invariably fly in, Victor-style, with no luggage and no passport.

In Philadelphia, he built Temple University's Humanities Building, and the $28 million Children's Hospital, another project that carried prestige and was a financial winner for Baltimore Contractors.

And yet Victor took these successes in stride, preferring to gamble on more risky ventures. Probably because these jobs were easy, he found them less challenging.

One of the risks was the Golden Sands project in Ocean City, Maryland. In the 1970s, he began to sell the apartments that were finished and ready for occupancy — just as the market became glutted and prices began to drop. The Golden Sands was an unusual job for him. Normally he did not build housing for sale, but the idea appealed to him perhaps because it was challenging and many of the political and contracting people he knew spent their summers in Ocean City. It was certainly a project that would afford exposure, just as Lyndon Johnson's assistant, Bobby Baker, got with his Carousel Motel, not far from the Golden Sands.

A hangar built by Baltimore Contractors at Andrews Airfield, Maryland.

The Golden Sands was a $10.5 million job that, because of an exculpatory cause, left Victor the option of walking away. He did not — and took it upon himself to sell all its units. While the odds appeared to be against him, this was the kind of challenge that appealed to his sense of daring.

In the end, he contacted all his friends, subcontractors and suppliers. He used all his powers of persuasion to convince them to buy a unit, more if necessary. They did and, if they held them long enough, realized excellent appreciation.

The June 1975 gala kickoff sale of the Golden Sands units gave Victor yet another publicity splash. He directed his public relations staff to gather the press and his faithful political friends from throughout the state. Many flew in on chartered planes Victor had engaged for the day. The dedication ceremonies drew a Jesuit priest, Fr. Daniel McGuire of Loyola College in Baltimore, who was quoted in an Associated Press story: "It's not just a condominium. It is a tower of human glory…an everlasting memorial to innovative organization —

a consecration to free enterprise".

The AP report said of the new owner: "Mr. Frenkil, 71, was introduced with a fanfare from a hired band. Hostesses served the guests, who ate and drank at Mr. Frenkil's expense". On hand were University of Baltimore president H. Mebane Turner and Maryland's Attorney General, Francis B. Burch, and State Comptroller Louis L. Goldstein. It was just like the old days at an Army-Navy game.

"I think Victor had an ego that kept him from being circumspect and discreet. I don't think he cared that people saw him as he actually was. He never tried to hide what he really was. He was totally at home with people. He liked to know them and he liked to be able to call on them, whenever he needed them," said Salvatore Manfre.

But by the 1970s the times were changing. No longer was the press as flattering. A *Baltimore Sun* editorial-page column by writer Peter A. Jay noted, "Mr. Frenkil, a Baltimore contractor who gets his jollies giving people money folded into shapes like their initials and who collects politicians the way some people collect baseball cards, has stuck a $20 million pleasure palace on the beach here that could be called an eyesore if it weren't surrounded by other eyesores equally grotesque".

The Golden Sands survived its detractors and naysayers, thanks to Victor's persistence. All the units sold. In fact, as competing condominiums were dropping their prices, Victor raised his. Once the real-estate recession lifted, the units quickly recovered their value.

The idea of retirement never occurred to Victor. He kept the same hours in 1980 as he did in 1930. And, late in his career, Victor overcame another serious setback. After doing business with the same bonding firm, United States Fidelity and Guarantee (USF&G) for 30 years, he found he could no longer get this insurer to stand behind him. This is what happened.

In July 1992, when he was nearly 84 years old, he recounted that Baltimore Contractors (BCI) had been then doing about $200 million worth of business a year.

In 1979, BCI bid and won the Dirksen-Hart Senate Office Building on Capitol Hill. It was a $35 million project and, in the words of the industry, the highly prestigious job (the building houses the personal offices of most of the U.S. Senate) that went bad, suffering costly and wholly unanticipated expenses.

At the time of the bidding, Victor said, the Architect of the Capitol did not disclose that the previous contractor had improperly placed anchor bolts on the perimeter walls. The Capitol Architect, which admitted the problem, then ran out of funds and authorized Victor's firm to appeal to Congress for recovery of its claim. In short, the Office of the Capitol encouraged BCI to seek an appropriation from Congress, a task that might take several years.

Complicating the task was the fact that politicians are naturally reluctant to risk any exposure in the press of subjects that could be construed as feathering their nests. And the overruns, of course, were caused in part by the sprucing up of the Senators' marble-clad offices.

Perhaps a more risk-averse (and wiser) contractor would have raised a red flag, stopped work, called in lawyers and walked away from the job. Not Victor. He prided himself on finishing what he started. This job, the office of the U.S. Senate, was probably his most prestigious and, if successful, would make an ideal cap to his long career in construction.

The result of these delays caused by the AOC created a ripple effect of time lost, cost overruns affecting all trades, suppliers and subcontractors, but primarily the steel erection and exterior marble work. The marble erector abandoned the job, which forced Baltimore Contractors to procure a substitute marble contractor at a substantially greater cost. Then severe winter weather conditions set in and the Senate Office Building had to be completely encased in a blanket of polyurethane.

Victor had a $12-million line

Baltimore Contractors also did extensive remodeling, this job for the New Theater in Baltimore.

of credit with three banks. The line got tapped out and he appealed to his bonding company, USF&G, for help. The firm had insured BCI for decades and Victor had enjoyed a close and friendly relationship with its management.

Until 1980, Williford Gragg, then president and CEO of USF&G, had advised Victor Frenkil. Chosen to succeed Gragg as president was Charles Foelber, then a senior executive-vice-president at the firm.

Two weeks later, while at a meeting in his office, Mr. Gragg introduced a newcomer, Jack Moseley, to Victor and advised him that in fact Mr. Moseley would be the new president. Victor Frenkil then made an impulsive blunder that would cost him dearly. He told the new man he favored Mr. Foelber for the job. Moseley, of course, never forgot this.

When the Dirksen-Hart's cost overruns tapped out Victor's line of credit, the new management at USF&G decided not to cooperate and support him or Baltimore Contractors. No matter that it had bonded him for more than 20 years.

The new management made no attempt to keep the company viable even though Victor pledged his good financial faith by putting all of his personal assets on the line. The bonding company seized Victor's assets and forced the liquidation of his personal holdings. In short, Victor was taken to the cleaners.

Victor prided himself on standing behind his work. In this regard, pledging all his personal assets was one of the many risks he was willing to take. While USF&G approved the money to complete the project, it nevertheless seized Victor's personal assets to make up the difference. Victor lost valuable real estate and other possessions in the deal. But, just as galling to him, was a decision the bonding company made not to press Congress for an additional $8 million in cost overruns. The bonding company refused to make a case for extra funds.

The Architect of the Capitol may have told Victor to seek the additional costs, but USF&G, for whatever reason, disagreed. Perhaps the bonding firm did not want to tangle with influential members of Congress. After all, this was not an appropriation for the military, or highways, or education. This was an additional charge for the senators' own offices, a much more sensitive subject.

USF&G then took the Senate Office Building project away from Baltimore Contractors and had it completed to the satisfaction of the federal government. And the bonding firm went after Victor and used his personal fortune to pay the debt.

As an outcome of this dispute, the insurer refused to back Baltimore Contractors again. A contractor without bonding cannot get work. The greatest damage was the word that spread within the insurance and bonding industry: "Do not insure Baltimore Contractors". Victor felt he was being black-balled. He could not function in the industry in which he had thrived for 50 years. For the first time in his professional career, Victor could not work. His men could not make estimates and his crews could not pour concrete.

For the next five years, Victor doggedly pursued other sources of bonding. He knocked on every door and eventually located some small insurers.

"As financially damaging as the Dirksen-Hart job was, the whole experience left him with a bad taste toward Jack Moseley. My father liked people and he did not like having enemies. I think he had an emotional thing about Moseley. It was a hard settlement. It left him with his business, but my father felt that USF&G took $40 million of his money to complete $20 million worth of work. He felt badly burned," said Victor Jr.

He persisted. Now in his 80s, he was hustling like he did when he was 20 and seeking contracts for front porches and bathrooms. One by one, he regained the confidence of the insurance industry. He never stopped working. He eventually emerged from this disaster as he had from other scrapes.

"He really revels in the realm of [Casey] Stengelese when the idea of retirement is brought up," noted a construction magazine article on Victor in 1976. The interview also caught Victor's speech patterns: "I would retire from this if…not having thought in that vein, that transition at this stage of the game must be in geometric rather than arithmetic terms. Having been at the helm in many areas and juggling several balls at the same time, it's not easy to turn over the reins in normal fashion. With these circumstances, I must make a choice in the next three years or so".

That was 1976 and in the 1990s he was still at work in his office at 711 South Central Avenue, surrounded by many of the people who would never leave his side.

At the time of his death, Victor had more than $100 million in jobs ready to be completed by his company, including lucrative cost-plus jobs from his reliable gypsum clients. "He had the ability to recover and come back from the depths of hell," said Victor Jr. "And the day he died, he left a company in excellent shape, full of business. He did not know the word quit."

To the end, the game was what mattered most to Victor, which is one of the chief reasons he learned to play it so well. Win or lose, he never stopped playing — until God finally took him out of the game.

XI. Beloved Folly

"Meet me at The Belvedere,
Come before the show.
Meet me at The Belvedere
And meet everyone you know..."
Victor Frenkil

In 1976, Victor Frenkil sent a personal message to everyone in Baltimore. It was short (five words), simple and memorable. It appeared on countless automobile bumpers in the form of an orange-and-black sticker with the words, "Meet Me at The Belvedere".

The phrase, actually the title of a song he composed celebrating the landmark hotel, could have been the story of his life for the decade and half he assumed the role of greeter, bon vivant and manager of the much-beloved 1903 hotel a few blocks to the north of Baltimore's Washington Monument. Victor, in fact, did want people to meet him at The Belvedere. After all, he fell in love with it, decided to save it, and bought it.

Today, the lone memorial to the investment of time, emotion and money that Victor lavished on the Belvedere Hotel is a collection of photos of him hanging in the corridor leading to its Owl Bar. He stands there with many of the prominent guests who stayed at The Belvedere through the years.

Victor poses with many, including President George H. W. Bush, First Lady Lady Bird Johnson, entertainer Harry Belafonte and South African civil-rights leader Archbishop Desmond Tutu. Yet these celebratory photographs do little to memorialize the man who did so much to restore the hotel to its former glory. Without Victor Frenkil, one of Baltimore's more amazing landmarks, visited by ten U.S. presidents, would have wound up demolished, converted into a parking lot or turned into low-income housing.

Friends said that Victor Frenkil worked harder and longer rebuilding and promoting The Belvedere than he did on any other project. His 15 years there earned him glowing publicity and the good will of many Baltimoreans who were relieved that one of their most loved landmarks had been rescued. As Victor's Belvedere took shape, he achieved the status of a courageous civic philanthropist, a resourceful master builder who could claim credit for brightening the city's aura after decades of negativity. Victor had dared to restore the landmark that the city's other influentials had allowed to deteriorate. And yet, for all his work, investment and years of attention, Victor's Belvedere ultimately wound up in the hands of the receivers. But it was not for lack of trying. And, he had a merry time playing innkeeper to Baltimore and its guests.

"He saw himself as an hotelier," said Vita Kencel, who worked at The Belvedere for a number of years when Victor owned it. "It brought glamour and he liked that. He liked being the center of attention and of showcasing what he could do. He would point to the place and say, 'Look what I did'."

In truth, The Belvedere, for all its grand balls, social pedigree and knockout plasterwork, was never a consistent moneymaker. It was constructed in 1903 and compared favorably to Philadelphia's Bellevue Stratford, Richmond's Jefferson and

On 20 October 1926, Queen Marie of Romania lunched at The Belvedere, then was presented to the city of Baltimore in War Memorial Plaza by Mayor Howard Jackson (on her left).

Washington's Willard hotels. Located nearly a dozen blocks uptown from the center of the business district in what had been a genteel residential quarter, it could claim visits by many dignitaries. It was where Woodrow Wilson stayed when he was nominated for President in 1912. Queen Marie of Romania had lunch there, as did most Hollywood stars in the golden era of film production. But long before Victor Frenkil came into the picture, the hotel was often in bankruptcy, and, by 1917, had passed through five different owners. Hotels can be notorious money losers.

In 1946 the Sheraton Hotel chain purchased The Belvedere, investing in the then 43-year-old property, and brought with it considerable reservation-booking power, thanks to the name Sheraton. The Belvedere enjoyed a measure of newfound prosperity (the Duke and Duchess of Windsor appeared there for a charity benefit in 1956), which was undercut by a misguided action of the city government in the middle 1960s. City planners, in their zeal for creating a new cross-town highway system, sketched an interstate highway through the Mount Vernon neighborhood and the block where the hotel sat. Sheraton officials reacted promptly and sold off the aging hotel, rather than have its rooms face the thoroughfare.

The Gotham chain bought the hotel and owned it from 1969 to 1971, hardly a good time in Baltimore's urban history because of the 1968 riots. The Belvedere closed as a hotel in June 1971 and was vacated a year later after a dismal period when the building became a makeshift college dormitory. The highway planned for the neighborhood was never built in its entirety, stopping several blocks to the west, leaving a battered ex-hotel with no prospects due to the massive infusion of cash needed to change its fortunes.

The closed hotel fell into the hands of its mortgage holder,

The Duke and Duchess of Windsor in the Windsor Suite at The Belvedere in 1957. The Duchess, of course, was the former Wallis Warfield of Baltimore.

the Monumental Life Insurance Company, an old Baltimore firm that sat just across the street from the hotel. The vacant hotel was a major liability and Monumental was anxious to sell it. One developer's plan to gut its historic interior and make it into cheap apartments evaporated in the middle 1970s when cost projections forecast trouble.

Victor's role in The Belvedere began quite by accident. In the fall of 1975, Monumental executives donated the old beds and furnishings to Goodwill Industries, which held a second-hand sale. This bazaar of old hotel bed frames, dressers and restaurant menus brought a flurry of nostalgic news articles that mourned the fate of the grande dame that had fallen on such hard times. Victor heard of the sale while looking for a large piano for the Golden Sands in Ocean City, whose condominium units he was still actively marketing.

"Victor called and said he was interested in the pianos," said James O'Conor Gentry, then the Monumental executive in charge of the hotel. "All the electricity was turned off in the building and the elevators were not running. The pianos were in the ballroom on the 12th floor. Victor started running up the stairs like a 20-year-old. Before the day was over, not only did he want to buy the pianos, but he wanted to buy and renovate the whole building. It was incredible."

The story of Victor wanting to buy the pianos and buying the building where they sat became instant Baltimore lore. He himself told it many times, always with great enthusiasm.

In the early days of his possession of the hotel, he and his attorney, John M. Jones, toured the hotel ballroom. Its windows were broken and its hardwood floors were covered in several inches of pigeon dung. Victor now faced the financial reality of turning around the landmark that everybody seemed to love, but nobody wanted to pay the cost of saving.

"Everyone told Victor The Belvedere would not be a money-maker," said Victor Jr. "Victor charged forward even before he got a loan. But, in the end, what he did for The Belvedere did more for him than anything else in his life."

It came as a surprise to readers of *The Sun* the morning of 1 January 1976. A page-one article had Victor Frenkil buying The Belvedere, promising to save and restore the landmark. In the past decade, his name had appeared in the paper connected to politics and questionable dealings. Now it was there for another reason, with him in the unusual role of city savior. It was a role mixed with success and failure.

Why The Belvedere? Victor Jr. believes it appealed to his father's penchant for challenge. The bigger the risk, the more he was drawn to the game. Victor also admired the actions of other individuals he saw as mentors. He watched his old friend, Chicago-based contractor Steve Heal, buy and renovate the Steven Hotel after he'd helped Victor on the Aquia Bridge project. After all, if Victor had built the Marylander Apartments, why couldn't he retrofit an old hotel? And while Victor was not an historic preservationist, he did personally enjoy salvaging old things, including real estate that was cheap and available. He had the ability to see value where others saw liability. Perhaps the property's low initial cost appealed to him. He paid $650,000 for the hotel, but wound up losing about $4.5 million over the next 15 years.

"My father had a salvager's blood in him. He could take something old and reuse it or fix it up so it would work," said Victor Jr. "Sometimes it cost him more than buying new, but he got a kick out of it and that was all that was important to him."

Throughout 1976 and 1977 Victor worked long and hard on The Belvedere, which he could see from his penthouse apartment at the Marylander, about 25 blocks north. If someone had left a light burning at night, Victor would call his night watchman to have it turned off. There was a mandatory-attendance staff meeting every Tuesday morning at 7:30, at which everyone from his chief lawyer to the rental agents and maintenance men were present. He did not like absences from these sessions. He also appointed one of his favorite and most efficient managers, Albert Ches, to run The Belvedere.

Through The Belvedere portal have walked many of the rich and famous of the world, from presidents to sports champions to famous actors and actresses.

When the engineers and architects told him the original 1903 stair towers did not meet safety code, he was forced to gut the marble and cast-iron steps. Victor had some of the marble saved and cut up as paperweights bearing the legend, "A Piece of The Belvedere". He gave them away by the thousands, as he did his "Meet Me at The Belvedere" bumper stickers.

He kept a supply of bumper stickers in his coat pocket. After the place opened, he paid his bellman to go through the garage and place stickers on every unstickered car there, whether the owners wanted it or not. When someone offered Victor a lift, he'd manage to place one of his adhesive calling cards on their bumper, too.

"My father personalized The Belvedere with his name," said Victor Jr. "He had a standing rule that every Saturday night, an officer of the company had to be present when The Belvedere would be crowded with banquets and people in the bar. He wanted nothing to go wrong and he wanted his presence to be felt."

Victor started work quickly. He hired well established architects, Cochran Stevenson and Donkervoet, and studied the city's list of historic and architectural guidelines that protected structures in landmark neighborhoods. He located Verna Rogers-Napier, the artist who painted the murals in the

Adlai Stevenson speaking in the 12th floor ballroom of The Belvedere on 24 September 1952 during his campaign for the presidency.

John Eager Howard Room in 1930s, and brought her back to Baltimore to inspect the still-surviving work of her youth. He was delighted when his second-born child, Vida, painted a portrait of John Eager Howard, the Revolutionary War general whose home stood near the hotel. Her painting still hangs above a large fireplace in one of the hotel's majestic public rooms.

"It was a very hard building to renovate, very costly. There were union problems, but the old structure was very strong," said Jerry Jarosinki. "And Victor was there very day. He had all kinds of good managers on the job but he thought he was more knowledgeable than they".

In 1977, Victor had two appraisers, Mac Gardiner and Harry E. Gilbert, assess the financial prospects for The Belvedere. Both agreed there was a market for upscale apartments in downtown Baltimore that was not being addressed. Because he had spent the last year or so selling condominium units in the Golden Sands, he felt he could rent apartments. After all, hadn't he owned and operated the Marylander?

He also correctly envisioned the business and revenue potential from the hotel's large public rooms and its bar.

Tapping his years of knowledge of construction, he acquired a little more property to the building's south and added a multi-story parking garage. While it had only about 450 spaces, the garage became one of the building's best assets and a strong source of revenue in an urban neighborhood where parking spaces were at a premium. He also gutted the hotel's basement coffee shop and made it into a mini-mall of shops, a Japanese restaurant called Nichi Bei Kai, and a luncheonette.

Perhaps his most imaginative use of the hotel's possibilities was on the 13th floor. There had been an old coatroom tucked under the building's Mansard-style roof. The coatroom functioned in conjunction with large parties held in the 12th floor's ballroom. His engineers found a way of opening this attic space and making it profitable, as the newly christened 13th Floor, a bar with spectacular views of the city. It was packed the day it opened and the crowds never stopped coming.

"The Belvedere was magnificent when Dad first opened it," said Victor Jr. "He really struggled with getting the building perfect and he kept fighting to make it that way. Projects that were easy just bored him. I think that's why he liked The

The Belvedere played host to Harry Belafonte on 13 January 1985, shown here with Victor Jr., Margaret and Victor.

Belvedere so much. During this period in his life, challenges were more important than merely making money. He needed action."

People who may have read of Victor Frenkil the political wheeler-dealer were now running into him, face to face, in The Belvedere lobby. There, under a canopy of glass chandeliers and Beaux Arts plasterwork, he stood, with that half smile and twinkle in his eyes. Perhaps the most flattering photo of Victor ever taken was made in the hotel's John Eager Howard Room. He rests his arm on a piano and appears thoroughly content (see page 204).

If any room was filled with memories, it was the hotel's bar, an amazing Arts and Crafts chamber designed in a rathskeller style. The walls were brick; the floor of glazed tile. Its long oak bar had never been modernized. The windows were circles of glass that resembled green bottles.

A pair of plaster owls sat atop the bar. They were the kind of dusty props that would have gone unsold for months in an antique shop, but these particular owls lent the room its unofficial name. These birds, for reasons that have never been established other than the power of local custom, stamped their name upon The Belvedere's bar, which became known as the Owl Bar or the Owl Room.

These plaster owls became a symbol for Victor's rescue of the hotel. His publicity man, Ed Hanrahan, devised a brilliant coup. During the time the hotel had closed, the original owls disappeared somewhere. In April of 1977, Mr. Hanrahan arranged to have them returned to their perch atop the bar, accompanied by free drinks to reporters and camera crews. The mysterious return of the owls was accompanied by a note that read: "Where we've been, what we've seen, no matter the din, no one will glean. But if your eyes are clear, today you can tell, the owls of The Belvedere have returned from hell".

"A group of seven veteran customers was brought together in the Owl Room, a pub in the hotel where they all put in a good number of hours in the Thirties, and Forties and Fifties and Sixties. The two owls, which stood on either side of the cash register in the old bar, had blinking yellow eyes but one pair was darker than the other. They were famous — so famous that a Second-World-War soldier returning home on leave, when asked what he wanted to see most in his native town, said he longed only to see those blinking owl eyes again," noted *The Sun* in 1977 under a headline "Highball to eyeball at The Belvedere".

The news report continued: "The brown birds were missing for six years, presumed stolen. They appeared this April 21, replaced by someone who apparently had crept through locked doors, set them on their perches and snuck out, leaving a rhymed calling card that shed no light on the mystery".

Carole Lombard and Clark Gable in Baltimore, 28 December 1940. The Gables always stayed at The Belvedere when in town.

As Victor turned 70 in 1978, he could point with pride to his considerable accomplishments at The Belvedere. In less than 18 months, he had achieved what others said would never happen. His apartments were being leased. The larger, more expensive ones leased the fastest, confirming his basic instinct that there was a market for quality rental residences in midtown Baltimore.

The first floor of The Belvedere became the meeting place for Baltimore. In the years before the city's Inner Harbor had taken off, The Belvedere was indeed the place to be. Every organization in town wanted to book its public rooms for meetings and banquets. Brides and their sponsoring fathers swooned over the grand ballroom and its adjacent assembly room. Victor, in this case, yielded to the advice of his architects and decorators. When The Belvedere reopened in 1977, it was a dazzler. He threw a series of opening parties, well attended by the press, who camped out at the free food tables and bars. The columnists who had taken pot shots at Ocean City and the Golden Sands were now eating their words, perhaps even forgiving, or, for the time being, forgetting about Victor's scrapes and troubles in the past.

Victor's investment in The Belvedere captured the attention of the press. A May 1979 *Baltimore Magazine* squib elevated him to the top ten of the city's "Biggest Big Shot" list. He shared the ranking with Mayor William Donald Schaefer, the owner of the Baltimore Orioles and the president of Johns Hopkins University.

The report stated: "When then-unknown state transportation secretary Harry Hughes resigned in protest against 'certain influences' affecting state contracts, he was talking about Frenkil. *The Sun* took up the charge with some characteristically nasty stories. As always, Frenkil landed on his feet. And he is now being lionized as the man who is restoring Baltimore's venerable Belvedere Hotel to its former glory."

For years Victor Frenkil rarely got home to the Marylander Apartments before 10 or 11 at night. The same was true now that he had The Belvedere, but at least its restaurants and bar afforded his wife Margaret a place where she could catch up with her husband. She knew where she could find him. The date-book diaries she carefully kept reveal just how often she had a "little snack" and a Scotch and soda at The Belvedere with him, maybe after she had attended an opera or play with other friends.

The same was true for the numerous Sunday brunches they hosted at the John Eager Howard Room, the baronial dining room that at times served as the main restaurant in the hotel. Margaret and Victor were often at one of the tables, a long-married couple who had never fallen out of love.

Victor and Margaret in the John Eager Howard room at one of the many parties at The Belvedere.

Victor enjoyed popular music and dancing. For a while, when he owned The Belvedere, he studied piano and musical composition. One of his many amateur efforts, meant to publicize the hotel and demonstrate his musical talents, was his song, "Meet Me at The Belvedere":

Meet me at The Belvedere,
Come before the show.
Meet me at The Belvedere,
And meet everyone you know.
Dining with society in a nook,
Mixing with celebrities

To take a second look.
There you'll meet your beaux
All dressed in fancy clothes.
They'll drink a toast to you.
At The Belvedere all who's who.
Meet me at The Belvedere, The Belvedere,
There I'll dance with you.
Meet me at The Belvedere.

"He and Margaret probably should have moved into The Belvedere and lived there in a nice centrally air-conditioned apartment," said Victor Jr. "But he stayed at the Marylander and lived with window units."

Victor, who often ate at restaurants, kept his eye on the food at The Belvedere. He initially engaged a local Baltimore firm, Gourmet Caterers. Several years later, he brought in the Pimlico Hotel's restaurant operators, Lenny and Gail Caplan. Ever the meddler, he fussed over food quality and service.

"He was never satisfied that the food was quite good enough," said Vita Kencel. "When he would go out to other restaurants, he would take a menu and fold it up and bring it back to The Belvedere, so he could describe a dish he felt we needed. He would also have me put a dinner roll from other restaurants in my handbag. When he returned, he would give the roll to our people and say, 'This was a very good roll'".

The Belvedere was placed on the National Register of Historic Places and Victor received the presentation on 15 September 1977.

Victor made The Belvedere a gathering point for stars and

noted personalities visiting Baltimore. He even managed to have himself filmed as a diner in a scene at the John Eager Howard Room when "And Justice for All," starring Al Pacino (who stayed at The Belvedere), was filmed in Baltimore. Victor's face is clearly visible in the released print. Throughout the 1980s he was photographed with Harry Belafonte, the mayors of Baltimore, college presidents and political cronies.

"There wasn't anything bad *The Sun* could say about The Belvedere," his son recalled of the run of favorable stories and publicity articles during the late 1970s and early 1980s.

In 1981, after The Belvedere had been up and running as an apartment house with several restaurants and bars, Victor, at the urging of then-Mayor William Donald Schaefer, borrowed additional city money to convert the apartments back into hotel rooms. The city was anxious to attract convention business, and Baltimore's hotel inventory was then not great enough to supply the needs of large convention goers.

Victor agreed to reconvert The Belvedere into a hotel. It proved an unwise move and was one he might not have taken were it not for his long-standing ties to Baltimore and its elected officials who were giddy over the success of their rebuilt Inner Harbor. He took a series of loans from the city to make The Belvedere into a hotel. The press described it as being about $3 million at the time. What Victor overlooked, or chose not to worry about, was the fact that The Belvedere was more than 12 city blocks up a hill from the harbor, which in the 1980s was fast emerging as the new downtown and the center of all convention business. Time has since proven that the center of Baltimore is its harbor. Nearly 25 years after Victor purchased The Belvedere, its neighborhood remains largely residential with many cultural attractions patronized by native Baltimoreans, not tourists and convention attendees.

"If I had to blame any failure on The Belvedere, it was its location," Victor Jr. said.

"The Belvedere had been going along very well as an apartment," said John M. Jones, then the attorney for Baltimore Contractors. "But as a hotel, the occupancy rates and the room rates were not enough to support The Belvedere."

In the 1980s there were political changes as well. Two strong Frenkil allies left local office. William Donald Schaefer was elected governor and moved on to the State House in Annapolis. His successor, Clarence Burns, held office only briefly before being defeated by Kurt L. Schmoke, an attorney who held no particular ties to Victor, who by this time owed the city about $5 million in loans and fees.

"He approached Schmoke 15 different ways," said Victor Jr. "My father honestly believed he had saved the Mount Vernon neighborhood. He had tax maps to show big increases in assessment."

No compromise was reached. In the spring of 1989, the corporation that controlled The Belvedere declared bankruptcy. "The sale of Baltimore's Beaux Arts gem of rococo columns and mansard roof was determined in the hush of a bankruptcy court. A judge more accustomed to deciding the fate of failing appliance stores and car dealerships shook his head and said there was nothing more to be done," *The Sun* reported in an article critical of both Victor and the city's loan trustees, who made loans to various projects, including other hotels, in the 1980s. When *The Sun* tabulated the losses the city sustained on its hotel investments in 1992, it reported The Belvedere lost $5 million, while the Lord Baltimore lost $7 million, the Omni Hotel lost $5.9 million and Harrison's Pier Six lost $11.6 million.

At the foreclosure sale, The Belvedere's creditors moved in.

Victor at the piano in the John Eager Howard room in 1986, where he frequently performed the songs he had composed. Above his head is the painting of Colonel John Eager Howard done by his daughter, Vida.

Victor attended the auction and was reported to be in good spirits. "Whoever ends up buying the hotel," he told a *Sun* reporter that day, "they got to live it and love it".

Many of the hotel's main public rooms closed during the bankruptcy reorganization. Victor Jr. rescued the pair of plaster owls from the bar and put them in storage. He later had them cleaned up and restored as a gift for his father. He took them to Victor's South Central Avenue office and presented them to him. By this time, The Belvedere had reopened as a condominium and the bar had a new owner.

"He kept the owls about a day and went back to The Belvedere and placed them on the bar," his son noted. "He said, 'They belong here'."

The owls are still there, along with the indomitable spirit of the Baltimorean who gave many years of his later life to his beloved folly, The Belvedere.

XII. The Philanthropist

"The more he gives to others, the more he possesses of his own."
Lao-tzu

Given Victor's demanding (and self-inflicted) schedule, he rarely saw his children in the evenings, so he often took them to school to have a chance to catch up with them. He frequently asked, "What good deed did you do yesterday?"

It was not an idle question. Throughout his life, Victor gave of himself to others. He enjoyed helping someone get an education, find a job or solve his or her financial troubles. His philosophy of charitable giving did not include public promotion of himself. He chose not to put his name on hospitals and college buildings, even though he had constructed many. His concept of a good deed was just that, an individual act of charity, perhaps performed daily, throughout an entire life, without fanfare. If the act of helping others helped Victor a little bit, then, he thought, so be it.

"He could not resist a beggar who asked for money," said his son, Victor Jr. "I occasionally got annoyed at him for giving away money like that, but he'd remind me that I didn't know the guy's story."

Victor liked to quote old saws that he wrote and repeated throughout his life. One of them was, "Don't ever throw money away. Instead, give it to charity. There are too many people out there in need".

Victor spent very little on himself. He was not impressed by name brands, hand-tailored suits, or flashy cars. The symbols of wealth that most people seek so assiduously and then display so consistently had no meaning for him. When it came to spending, his focus was on those around him who needed help.

It is hard to say when Victor's good deeds began but, by December of 1944, he was already getting some notice of his work. An article in *The Sun* about Baltimore Contractors was headlined, "Every Employee of this firm is a Santa Claus". It reported how Victor asked that all the employees furnish him with the name and address of a needy family, of orphaned children, of widows with little or no income, or of the aged and infirm. That year Baltimore Contractors helped some 400 of the disadvantaged with baskets of Christmas goodies that included coffee, marmalade, syrup, pancake flour, wheat flour, potatoes, lettuce, cabbage, turnips, string beans, celery, a box of candy, loaves of bread, oranges, apples, dried beans and peas, a box of tomatoes and chicken. The story also called Victor "the Number One Santa".

Victor continued this holiday tradition throughout his life, sending an annual Christmas reminder in the fall to his staff and subcontractors. He would supply the contents of the baskets. His one rule was that they had to deliver them personally.

For nearly six decades, Victor supported the American Cancer Society through his dollar-bill folding. No tabulation could be made of how much he donated, or in reality, caused to be donated. Like much of what he did, this form of charity had his personality imbedded upon it. When Victor made a person's initials and mailed the memento to them, he enclosed a letter asking the recipient to make a donation to the American Cancer Society. His secretaries, led by Virginia Lambrow, kept detailed records of who had been mailed dollar bills. It was up to the recipient to make the donation to the American Cancer Society. Judging by the correspondence retained in the Baltimore Contractors' files, many, if not most of the persons for whom Victor folded bills, donated to the charity. Oftentimes, they gave $5 for the dollar bill he gave them. (For many years Victor took a tax deduction on his federal income tax form for his dollar-bill folding. Though he was frequently [and closely] audited by federal authorities in his later life, the amount was never challenged.)

World War II and the Korean War were times when the country pulled together in a united effort. Medical and other charities were calling on local businesses and their employees for donations. This was the sort of work Victor loved. He set up various fund-raising committees and stressed that they were competing with one another.

He held special meetings, luncheons and dinners, all of which afforded him the chance to make new acquaintances, fold dollar bills and, in his own mind, get "exposure" as he raised money. There were not many non-religious charities in Baltimore during the period that Victor did not support and, more important, have an active hand in organizing.

"Develop and maintain the right image," Victor would often say. "Without a good image, you can't stay in business." This could be a reference to many things, including a neat and orderly job site as well as a visible public role in organized giving.

Margaret and Victor in formal dress at one of the many charity affairs they supported, not only by sponsoring but also by attending.

He appeared at the old Southern Hotel for the opening of the 1950 Cancer Crusade in Maryland as chairman of the trade and industry division. He told his committees to go at it "with a bang". A few months later, he reported that his Red Cross construction division had topped its projected giving by 120 percent.

He became the volunteer chairman of the 1953 Baltimore March of Dimes' Corporation and business committee. News stories said he pledged his group to raise $80,000, twice as much as the previous year. Victor told reporters he was motivated to up the contribution goal because of increases in polio outbreaks (he was still a fairly young father who would have worried about his children and this dreaded disease). As the chair for the entire Baltimore business community, he regularly attended meetings with everyone from the managers of the city's largest hotels to automobile plants and commercial bakeries, working his sub-chairmen with handshakes, folded dollars and business cards.

Other newspaper accounts report that he led drives for underprivileged children at the *News-Post* Kiddies' party and private drives for the aged in the municipal hospital. He gathered gifts for bone-injured children at Kernan Hospital at Easter. He even funded a $150 annual Victor Frenkil Prize for the best original television script. The award was administered by Johns Hopkins University and, later, the University of Maryland. It was a curious award that lasted about six years. (Given Victor's impatience, it is questionable whether Victor himself would have sat still for a one-hour television drama were any of the scripts actually performed.)

Accolades followed. In 1954, he was named Man of the Year by the Marine Corps American Legion's Post No. 1. General Earl Waldron presented him with a bronze plaque for "human kindness of dynamic leadership, faith in his fellow man and generosity of outlook which inspired and enriched the community of which he is so vital a part". The general noted how Victor had begun by fixing up houses some 20 years before and had run "a $300 investment into I don't know how many millions". Yet, the general said, "He never forgot that he, too, is just a guy".

The United States Internal Revenue Post of the American Legion presented an annual "certificate of outstanding citizenship" for his "contribution to public and private charity" in 1951. The engineering society, Phi Alpha, put him on the cover of its magazine and named him 1953's distinguished alumnus.

His activism in community issues was not limited to ordinary charity. He flirted with becoming a professional sports tycoon. In 1949, he floated an offer to buy and revive the aging Pimlico Race Course, home of the Preakness Stakes, although not much came of the offer (the course was purchased by his friends, Herman and Ben Cohen). He also got on the promotional bandwagon for the young Baltimore Colts franchise and, after an early Colts victory, threw a lavish party at his Wilton country home that won praise from the sports columnists.

He was elected to the board of the brotherhood of the Har Sinai, his religious congregation in June 1949, and several months later became its house committee chair. In 1952, he was a member of the board that was then in the process of building a Jewish Community Center on Park Heights Avenue. He also built Chizuk Amuno Congregation's social and educational center. Throughout his life he was a large donor to what was then the Associated Jewish Charities.

He also believed in the principles espoused by the Boy

Scouts of America and made numerous donations to it. Through a foundation he initiated (this time in his name), he was generous to the urban parochial schools of Baltimore, Beth Jacob Congregation, the Chesapeake Center for Youth Development, Junior Achievement, the Rotary, Masonic charities and his neighborhood Roman Catholic church, SS. Philip and James, where a memorial was created in his and Margaret's names after their deaths.

Although Victor loved music, it is doubtful he ever sat through an entire symphony or opera performance (his definition of "music" was not that inclusive). Yet, when asked to help the Baltimore Symphony Orchestra, he agreed and then worked his magic as a string puller and fundraiser. It was in 1955 (as he was working for his medical charity campaigns), when he got a call from a friend who was greatly concerned. The Baltimore Symphony Orchestra was $160,000 in debt. Its current treasurer was unable to raise the money to pay it off, and it looked as if the symphony might fold. Working with Johns Hopkins surgeon and gynecologist, Dr. C. Bernard "Bozo" Brack, Victor launched one of his intense string-pulling campaigns.

Victor agreed to join the symphony's board as its treasurer, a post that was not the kind of task he would normally seek. "It was almost as hard to be treasurer of the Baltimore Symphony as it was to be president of Baltimore Contractors," he later admitted.

He recalled, "Dr. Bozo Brack and I took on the task together, he as president, and I as treasurer. Many a time we had to use money that wasn't really ours. Once we even used funds that belonged to the federal government, Social Security payroll taxes. But, as luck would have it, we made it".

It wasn't luck, it was hard work. The solution to the immediate cash shortfall was a $100-a-plate dinner held at the Lord Baltimore Hotel. Behind the scenes, Victor and others lobbied the Maryland General Assembly for a one-time donation of $50,000.

Newspaper stories noted that Victor sold $10,000 worth of tickets to the save-the-symphony dinner at the Hotel. Metropolitan opera diva Rosa Ponselle, who had moved to Baltimore some years previously, raised $5,000. Sports official Larry MacPhail, his co-chairman, raised $6,000. This venture into the cultural arts of Baltimore brought him even more of the exposure he liked to cultivate; his name was now appearing prominently among the city's civic leaders. MacPhail was quoted in the *News-Post* saying that Victor Frenkil did all the work and he (MacPhail) got all the publicity.

Victor used these associations to build friendships. At the symphony, he worked with Dr. Frank C. Marino, a surgeon who liked to spend time in civic works. Victor put Dr. Marino on his board of directors at Baltimore Contractors. They remained close associates.

Victor also helped the Baltimore Civic Opera Company when it was in one of its financial hiccups. The opera needed a well known star to sell tickets. At the time, John Charles Thomas was a draw and a favorite of Baltimoreans. Victor agreed to underwrite the entire production, including Thomas' fee. He also put up $6,000 in cash to help defray the opera's operating costs until the opera's balance sheet improved.

While Victor thrived on the attention that charity and arts fund-raising brought, he truly believed in the lasting value of education. Throughout his life, if he could help a student, employee or friends better themselves through a college course or degree, he did it. Victor liked being an active participant in his good deeds. He also liked finding worthy recipients.

For example, on one Martin Luther King Day celebration at the Belvedere, with Rosa Parks and Stevie Wonder in attendance, he met a young musician named David Alan Bunn. Before the night was over, Victor asked the student to give him piano lessons at his home in the Marylander Apartments. Victor soon had a regular Saturday morning appointment. "Victor was responsible for my advanced musical education," David Bunn said. "He was so incredibly encouraging to me, saying that I could meet my goals."

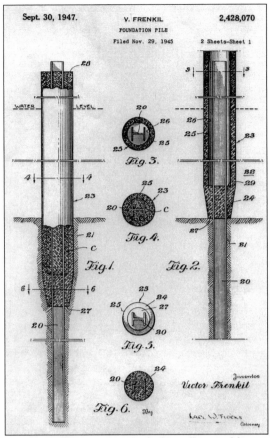

Victor created a novel method of installing steel beams with the upper beams encased in concrete, providing prefabricated concrete encasements for steel beam piles. This simplified installation, saved time and money. A patent was granted 30 September 1947, and Victor donated the invention to the construction industry.

Victor paid Mr. Bunn's tuition to study music at the Fontainebleau in France. The additional studies helped the young musician get a job working with New York theater musician and conductor Luther Henderson.

Their friendship continued, as did Victor's help. Victor assisted the young man when his grandmother needed medical treatment and felt that her doctors were not giving her proper care. Victor, ever the man with contacts, called friends at Johns Hopkins. The woman had an operation shortly thereafter and lived another decade.

Victor had a standing policy at Baltimore Contractors that any employee who took a course would be reimbursed, based upon attendance and grades received. As the head of Baltimore Contractors, Victor handed out a questionnaire to his employees that asked where their outside interests lay. When some answered "nothing", he tried to get them involved in the life of the community.

He was a soft touch when employees had financial or personal family issues. He would give jobs to his employees' relatives, hire legal counsel, provide medical care, pay for children's education, and call in political debts from judges and elected officials to help families in trouble. Many of these acts were anonymous. But, as employees spoke among themselves, they spread his reputation as a benevolent surrogate father. This was one of the reasons Baltimore Contractors had a low turnover rate.

His focus on education had roots in the Forest Park High School experiences of his youth. Because of his dyslexia, he could never get the grades of his classmates or brothers and sisters. Yet, on the strength of his personality, he was one of the leaders of the senior class, and was coached and tutored by sympathetic faculty members, including Ruth Kramer and Bill Jolly, with whom he maintained longtime friendships. (More than 50 years after his graduation from Forest park, Miss Kramer was a frequent guest at the Frenkil table.)

Victor funded two annual scholarships at Forest Park. One

was in his name; the other in that of Rex Simms, his sports coach with whom he also maintained a long friendship. Victor made many trips back to his high school. He returned, for example, in 1947, to congratulate Leon Schwartz, who established a new quarter-mile running record that year, thus besting Victor's own 1927 mark, of which he was so proud. When the school celebrated its golden anniversary, Victor was there at the reunion parties. And, in 1996, some 67 years after he had left the school, he returned to its stage to make the senior scholarship awards. By this time, the surrounding Forest Park neighborhood had gone through ethnic and demographic change. Of course, Victor would have known none of the students. Yet, he believed in them and their education. His files, maintained by Virginia Lambrow, show the correspondence he kept up with those who won his scholarship.

He was also asked to help students with their final payment of class

Ruth Kramer, the woman who helped Victor succeed at Forest Park High School, whom Victor later helped throughout her life.

expenses, graduation and college application fees. "The students are mostly from single-parent homes, and some of them are almost self-supporting and have jobs awaiting them upon their graduation from Forest Park," a school staff member wrote to Victor in 1996. Victor paid their bills.

In his later life, Victor contributed substantially to the United Negro College Fund, a charity which he believed would go a long way to help promising black students. Those he helped enrolled at St. Augustine's College, Virginia Union University, Clark Atlanta University, where they studied social work, finance, and biology. All were Baltimore city residents.

He was generous to Loyola College in Baltimore, where he developed a friendship with its president, the Rev. Joseph Sellinger. He also helped with a Goucher College fund-raising campaign when the school was moving to a new campus in Towson.

His 1999 obituary quoted Dr. Calvin Burnett, president of Coppin State Teachers College, a historically black school, as saying that Victor had been one of the school's most generous benefactors.

"He was the best friend we ever had," Dr. Burnett said. "Mr. Frenkil did not approach an institution to give him a name. He would take his name to the institution. When he believed in something, he really believed. He was unshakable."

"He clearly understood what Coppin was trying to do and I would estimate that, over the years, he gave $500,000 to the institution," Dr. Burnett said. "When it came to Coppin, he had a heart of gold."

Victor's affection for education and his political connections landed him a lengthy tenure on the Board of Trustees of the State Colleges, beginning in the mid 1960s. It was a post he took seriously and devoted long hours to its meetings,

From left to right: Rabbi David Holtz, Senator Paul Sarbanes, Archbishop William Keeler, Louis Goldstein, Victor Frenkil. Victor was extremely generous to both the Jewish and Catholic communities in Baltimore.

(where, of course, he sat quietly and folded dollar bills). Appointed by his friend, Governor J. Millard Tawes, he presided over Maryland's colleges and universities during the tumultuous 1960s, when thousands of Flower Children and Woodstock regulars were going off to college. He sat on the board until his term expired in 1978.

In his recollections of the period, Victor remembered how one of the state's black schools, Bowie State College, had fallen on hard times: Its academic standards had plummeted and its finances were in peril. There were those who were calling upon the state to close the school. The students were outraged and staged a sit-down strike. They demanded that Governor Spiro T. Agnew (Governor Tawes' term of office was over and Victor was still on the board) come to their campus and hear their side of the story. Agnew initially refused to go. The contention continued. Finally, when he realized the problem wasn't going away, Agnew called a meeting of the college's trustees, board and several prominent educators and business persons. As a board member, Victor was invited and addressed the governor (who would later be chosen by Richard M. Nixon as his running mate): "Do you want to hear the truth or do you want to hear what you want to hear?" Agnew flushed and said, "The truth".

"Ted, you should have had the guts to go down there and shake hands with those kids, the way Jack Kennedy would have done. They wanted to talk to somebody in authority, a big shot. That should have been you, but you didn't do it. If you'd gone, the criticism of the system wouldn't have reached this level," Victor recalled saying.

Then Victor made a passionate plea for additional funding, outlining the mission of the school and its potential impact upon the future of the state. When he sat down, there was dead silence. Everything relevant had been said.

Stung by these words, Governor Agnew was anxious to mend his fences with Frenkil and the other board members, all of whom were unhappy with the financial support the college had received. Like Victor, they were convinced it was a neglect grounded in unconscious racism. But he was the one who stood up, looked Governor Agnew in the eye, and told him the hard truth.

After the meeting, Agnew called a special meeting of the Bowie State College Board and made additional funds available, a quick fix of $300,000. This allocation took care of the immediate problem and the college began to rally. Under the guidance of a dynamic president, Dr. Samuel L. Myers, the academic standards were substantially raised. Gifts and appropriations increased.

In a few years, Bowie was on its feet again and it was announced that its commencement speaker would be Victor Frenkil. Instead of talking of vague generalities about the future, Victor talked very specifically about the past. He told students exactly how Bowie had been lifted from its academic and financial doldrums, and he named names, including that of the then Vice-President of the United States, Spiro T. Agnew. The students gave him a rousing ovation.

In 1966, Victor was given a testimonial dinner at the Belvedere Hotel. He was honored for his fund-raising work for the National Jewish Hospital in Denver, Colorado. Now 58, the news stories that accompanied this honor added to his image of civic philanthropist, a term used prominently in his obituary many years later. At that time, he was associated with the March of Dimes, the Red Cross, Hillel, the Big Brothers of Baltimore, the American Cancer Society and the Baltimore Opera. He was a trustee of the North Charles General Hospital, a favorite charity of his close friend James Swartz. He sat on the board of the Levindale Hebrew Home, and the board of governors of St. John's College in Annapolis.

Jimmy and Laura Swartz. Jimmy was Victor's mentor, his best friend, and a significant influence on the person Victor became.

A headline in *The Sun* referred to him as a "1-Man Foundation," while the accompanying article commented, "Organized charity is easy to get inspired about, but I don't know anybody who does what he does on the side. He's a one-man Rockefeller Foundation. How many students have had scholarships, how many businesses have had help — paid or pried loose by Mr. Frenkil? Not even Mr. Frenkil knows".

Then the article quoted him as saying that charity is a lot like business: "As you do one job for one person, they recommend you to somebody else," he said. The article ended by saying, "But in charity, unlike business, Mr. Frenkil lets someone else balance the books".

When the books of Victor's life were balanced at his death, there is little question but that any deity would have welcomed this remarkable, self-made, controversial, giving, headstrong, unusually kind human into its fold.

XIII. THE
COMING OF AGE

"Because I could not stop for Death,
He kindly stopped for me —
The Carriage held but just Ourselves
And Immortality."

Emily Dickinson

A ge was something that had no meaning for Victor, a
detail that was unconsciously brushed aside by the
demands of doing what he loved to do most — competing to keep building Baltimore Contractors.

As he moved into his eighties, he kept working with virtually the same energy with which he had always been blessed.
He awakened early, had breakfast and sped off to work, arriving well before most employees who were less than half his age.

He kept up the same business ties that had been the pillars
of his earlier successes, creating new ones as less-fit contempo-
raries fell by the wayside. Baltimore Contractors remained
viable; in the late 1990s Victor and his loyal staff were ready to
embark on a major job, and were making plans for the kind of
heavy work that characterized the business for more than six
decades.

221

Victor and best friend Jimmy Swartz at the Marylander, 3501 St. Paul Street. No doubt the men had left the ladies inside to slip out onto the terrace for a private chat about some pending business deal or political campaign.

In spite of his age, he had a won a $90-million cost-plus job for a gypsum plant, plus the new Ripkin baseball stadium in Harford County, and a new Northern District police station in Baltimore.

Victor was fortunate in having a strong constitution. He simply willed it. Over the years, his diet was terrible: he loved fatty foods, but he never smoked and rarely drank. His constant activity, powered by endless nervous energy, was a substitute for exercise. And occasionally he ran laps at the Gilman

School — if he was accompanied by friends who not only kept him company but also offered newsy tidbits. After they ran, Victor invited his friends back to the Marylander, where Margaret would cook a big breakfast for all.

Eventually his heart began to give out. One night just before his 90th birthday, he had dinner with his brother, James, feasting well on a suckling pig at Tio Pepe's restaurant, something he had been doing for years. Very early the next morning, he awakened with chest pain and immediately diagnosed that he was having a heart attack. He called his brother James (a doctor), who advised him to get to a hospital immediately. Victor dressed in a coat and tie, walked downstairs to the apartment lobby, went out to the street and hailed a cab, telling the driver to take him to the hospital.

Things got confusing. James, his brother, logically thought that Victor would leave the Marylander's back door, cross Calvert Street and go to the nearby Union Memorial Hospital, so close in an emergency — and within sight of Victor's home. But to Victor, personal connections had been the factor in his life that had given him the greatest leverage, and in this life-threatening moment, personal connections outweighed proximity. So he told the driver to take him to Johns Hopkins Hospital, where he knew he could count on his good friend, Dr. Levi Watkins, a renowned cardiologist whom Victor had met years before when Dr. Watkins had been one of his tenants at the Belvedere.

James went to Union Memorial and found no one registered under the Frenkil name. So he immediately called Victor Jr., who, understanding his father better, picked up James and together they found him in the Johns Hopkins emergency room.

Victor recovered from the heart attack. But it left him weak and with diminished circulation, which required surgery to improve the flow of blood to his toes.

"My father was never an old man until his heart attack," said Victor Jr. "After years of fighting he was always able to come back, but this blow really slowed him down."

Victor may have slowed, but he did not stop. His son, Leonard, with whom he worked at Baltimore Contractors, had a chair lift installed so Victor could get to his second-floor office and continue to work. He was able to put in a full day, even if he tired more easily.

Victor turned 90 in September of 1998. His family threw him a birthday party at the Center Club, attended by many old friends, including many of the notables who had been present at lawn parties, trips to an Army-Navy game and com-

Victor caught in a reflective mood at his office of many years on the water-front at Baltimore Contractors in January of 1986.

Probably the last photograph taken of Victor and Margaret Frenkil, not too long before they both reached the end of an unusually successful relationship.

pany banquets.

He arrived in a wheelchair, received his guests, but, energized by a standing ovation, got to his feet and led a chorus of "Meet Me at the Belvedere".

The master of ceremonies was Hopkins surgeon Levi Watkins. The speakers included former Governor William Donald Schaefer, who recalled Victor's uncanny ability to get President Lyndon Johnson on the phone. There were judges present: Dulaney Foster, Robert Watts and Anselm Sodero. Long-time city budget director Charles Benton spoke (he called Victor his "best friend", as did Chuck Gaston of the Small Business Administration). Roman Catholic pastor

Victor in his later years at home, pursuing one of his favorite hobbies: composing music, which he would then sing merrily at the slightest provocation.

William Au gave the blessing. Among the many guests were Virginia Lambrow, Sal Manfre, Tony Weir and George McManus.

His brother James spoke of what it was like having Victor as the older sibling. Dr. Watkins read birthday greetings from Baltimore's Archbishop William Keeler, Archbishop Desmond Tutu, poet Maya Angelou and Coretta Scott King.

A video recording of the night shows him rallying to the occasion and becoming the old Victor again. All present agreed it was a grand evening.

Sadly, Margaret could not be at his side. Her health had failed years before. For some time, she had been beset by severe hip pain. Ever the cheerful patient, she had three operations for hip replacements, the first done while she was in her 60s. The procedure proved effective for about a dozen years. During the last hip replacement, which took place at

Children's Hospital (where she had volunteered her time for decades), she was kept under anesthesia for 11 hours while the hospital and its staff searched for an implant device, a prosthesis that should have been shipped from the Washington suburbs but, for some reason, had not been ordered in advance. In addition, the joint had been repaired previously with a bonding epoxy; the orthopedic surgeon who performed the surgery told Victor Jr. that it took extra time to scrape and remove this compound. This required an additional period under the anesthesia, which left her weakened.

Shortly thereafter, she developed Alzheimer's disease and had to be confined to her home in the Marylander, cared for by nurses for the last ten years of her life.

The rhythm of life changed at the Marylander. Margaret was no longer capable of making a meal at whatever hour Victor returned home. Rather than give up what had been their home for 40 years, Victor found a devoted and efficient caregiver who was a registered nurse, Evangeline Horton, who kept house, shopped, prepared meals and looked after Margaret.

Family members recalled that it was now Victor who needed to assume some of Margaret's duties as mother, grandmother and great-grandmother, at which point he finally realized the painstaking work that went into her extensive attention and devotion to the family. He was impressed by her meticulously filed index-card system that kept track of the birthdays and anniversaries of all the family members as well as dozens of business associates.

When the end came, it was Evangeline Horton who called Victor Jr. to say that his mother was dying. Margaret succumbed 12 October, 1998, about a month after Victor's 90th birthday celebration. Victor Jr., was at her side, along with

Evangeline Horton.

Her funeral, a remembrance of Margaret's unconditional love, was held at Sol Levinson and Sons. She was eulogized by her Roman Catholic pastor, Father William Au, her daughter, Janet, and a grandson, Leonard Frenkil, Jr. Victor's rabbi, Floyd Herman, also prayed and offered the Psalm, "The Lord Is My Shepherd". Father Au asked for a prayer of thanksgiving "for the relationship that we shared for over six decades. Out of the love for him she raised her children in the traditional faith of Israel, while in her own heart she kept her own Christian faith and taught her own children the respect and tolerance for all people that love demands".

"Victor never tired of talking about Margaret," Father Au said. "He depended upon Margaret to take care of things, to make the home work, to take care of the charitable giving for the family...The ones most important and dear to her heart had to do with children, especially young children...Victor never tired of talking about how she was first and foremost that loving mother."

Her first-born child, Janet, spoke of her parents' love and respect for each other and of her mother's great, non-judgmental support. She said there was never a qualifier to Margaret's love. "It was the wind behind the sail of Dad's ship that never expected recognition. It was a warm wind that kept the family on an even keel — a wind that never blew too hard. It was a gentle source of power...."

Janet recalled her mother's ability "to be pleasant and interested without being Pollyannaish or aggressive". She recalled that, in all their time together, she could only remember her mother raising her voice once. She spoke of Margaret's patience and serenity in her last years. She also recalled how Margaret and her close friend Monica McGeady often

A memorial bench placed next to the grave in which Margaret is buried at Har Sinai Cemetery. It was inscribed to capture her most endearing characteristic: "The love of giving, the gift of love".

exchanged gifts of violets throughout their many years of friendship.

There were 14 bunches of violets on the casket to symbolize her 14 grandchildren.

Representing her grandchildren was Leonard Frenkil, Jr., who spoke at length of a grandson's admiration for a very special person. It was a speech that artfully and emotionally encapsulated Margaret's magnetic hold on people. In a speech that only a grandson could give about a beloved grandmother, he said: "She was beautiful, graceful and elegant. There was a glow about her … people would be attracted to her. As a child, you wondered if she were a celebrity".

Her grandson recalled her smile, "which lifted your spirits and brightened your day. You knew she was concerned". He remembered vividly the hundreds of index cards she kept which contained names, addresses and significant dates. He recalled that all these records "seemed mechanical," but of course were a manifestation of Margaret's devotion and careful attention — a precision that served her well in business and in social affairs.

The cards she mailed were penned "in her distinctive and exquisite handwriting" and mailed with special stamps, never an ordinary stamp bought in a grocery store. She went to the main post office and bought commemorative issues which "she procured with great interest". For her grandchildren, she also liked "Love" stamps. She always included "a note, a phrase of encouragement" to make everybody feel special.

"When night came and the family was fed and settled in, she began knitting mile after mile of bandages for lepers." He would have had no way of knowing it, but that charity was a Roman Catholic mission in India run by the Society of Jesuit, or Jesuits. For many years she and her friend, Ruth Kramer, knitted bandages of a type that could be washed and reused at the Indian leper colony.

"She worked to constantly improve the world for everyone," Leonard Jr. said that day.

Her grandson also stated she was a great matriarch and was the center of the immediate family, as well as that of all the extended Frenkils, Victor's brother and sisters, their children and the family of her own clan, the Panzers. Her love, of course, extended to the stepfamily members as well.

Margaret was laid to rest in the family plot at Har Sinai Cemetery. It was one of the few times that both a rabbi and a priest conducted services at the same burial, a reflection of the manner in which Margaret Frenkil embraced the two religious traditions.

Victor felt the loss deeply. Now without the faithful partner who had sustained him for nearly seven decades, Victor Frenkil succumbed less than eight months later, on June 3, 1999. A patient at Levindale Hebrew Geriatric Center for several weeks, he died at nearby Sinai Hospital.

The funeral was held the next day in the sanctuary of the Har Sinai Congregation. Its pews were filled with many of the people Victor helped during his life, including William Donald Schaefer, former Baltimore City Council president Walter Orlinsky and a long list of judges, contractors and other Maryland notables.

The memorial bench next to Victor's grave at Har Sinai, inscribed to summarize the man he was: "The day shall not be up so soon as I, To try the fair adventure of tomorrow" (from Shakespeare's "King John").

After an introduction by Rabbi Floyd Herman, his grand-children Jean Frenkil Ayres and Jeff Krieger; his brother, Dr. James Frenkil; cardiologist and friend, Dr. Levi Watkins; and a trusted and loyal employee, Sal Manfre, spoke.

Jean Frenkil Ayres, the seventh grandchild, spoke first, fol-lowing Rabbi Herman's remarks and prayers. She entitled her remembrance, as the seventh grandchild, "The Five Lessons" her grandfather had taught her:

Lesson One: "Give to others". She recalled how Victor would give to those who shared his ideology and to those who did not. He gave, with great generosity, his time, his wisdom, all "with great humility".

Lesson Two: "Follow your dreams". With considerable insight into her grandfather's personality, she recalled how he'd set a track record at high school that lasted for many years, res-cued a Baltimore landmark and learned to play the piano in his sixties. "With great conviction, he realized them," she said of a life in which he'd relentlessly pursued goals in the face of obvi-ous obstacles.

Lesson Three: "Establish tradition". She recalled a grandfa-ther, a patriarch in the middle of a family, in red pajamas at Christmas, at Barren Island on Thanksgiving, and with a silver dollar at Passover Seder. She recalled his "anchor of stability" at all those family gatherings at which each child and grandchild with each repeated custom was drawn into a circle of love.

Lesson Four: "Enjoy life". She recalled how Victor, in the hospital after his recent heart attack, sent out for a lobster din-ner, no matter how much bother and disruption it caused. "He loved to play," she said. "He also played hard at life." When he accompanied his grandchild to the circus — an event he savored — "He ate the most, gasped the most, and stared wide-eyed the most". He also took a delight in playing the

232

The tombstone shared by Margaret and Victor in Har Sinai Cemetery on the outskirts of Baltimore, where, after sixty-six years of married life, the two lie together in eternal peace.

game of Follow-the-Leader, as a Pied Piper leading 14 grand-children through restaurant kitchens and under tables.

Lesson Five: "Make a difference". She spoke of Victor's consuming passions. "There was no arena in which he did not make a difference," she said, be it in business or family.

Jeff Krieger, the eldest grandson, spoke next. He picked up his cousin's theme and added four more lessons:

Lesson Six: "Tolerance". Jeff Krieger spoke of Victor's rebelling against the intolerance and the injustice that often accompany racial and religious differences. "Accept people for their words and deeds," he said.

Lesson Seven: "Pride". Victor beamed a big smile for his family. "He was proud of the bridges he built, the people he met, the songs he wrote...He lived a long life, nearly the entire century. He taught us to succeed without being arrogant."

Lesson Eight: "Age is No Obstacle to Learning. He seemed to run out of time to accomplish all he wanted to do," his grandson said, adding never to rest in our efforts to better ourselves.

Lesson Nine: "Treasure Your Family. He truly delighted in a large and close family," Jeff Krieger said. "They were the grandparents every child wanted to have." He recalled Victor's adoration of and devotion to Margaret and how he had been the "epicenter" of the Frenkil family.

Dr. James Frenkil came next. He spoke in a relaxed and conversational tone. He told family stories and added a nice touch of humor. He told of how Victor invariably called him every night about midnight. One time, the phone rang and James inquired, "What do you want, Vic?" He responded, "How did you know it was me?" The mourners broke into knowing laughter. Dr. Frenkil then told a series of charming anecdotes about Victor's compelling personality, of his ability to put his feet up on the principal's desk at Forest Park High School, of how he could get others to work for him — and work harder, of how, when brother Jim broke his collarbone at football, Victor hid him in the cellar so his mother wouldn't notice. It was a sincere and intimate portrait of brotherly love.

Dr. Levi Watkins, the Johns Hopkins cardiologist who had looked after Victor, also spoke: "Every now and then a man is born who stands ten feet tall over other men, a man who refuses to give up on other people," a man who "espouses popular causes at unpopular times".

"He used to tell me, 'Levi,'" the doctor recalled, "'there is

234

The Margaret and Victor Frenkil Sanctuary Wing, seen from the outside and the inside at Har Sinai Synagogue in Owings Mills, donated in loving memory of them by their children.

no right way to do a wrong thing'. Typical Vic wisdom."

"Every now and then a man is born whose vision exceeds his reach," he said of Victor, then added, "Joy is work and work is joy". He remembered a few of Victor's sayings: "Do it now. Don't wait for tomorrow. Keep your eye on the ball. Do you have the ball?" He also spoke of Victor's lifelong passion for Baltimore Contractors and its employees and how, should someone fall sick, he'd call, concerned, "at three A.M. as if you needed heart surgery".

Dr. Watkins, who lived at the Belvedere, recalled the story of Victor's going into the darkened hotel to buy a used piano. "He saw not the piano, but a light of empowerment for the whole Mount Vernon area."

"I'll miss you. I'll miss those five A.M. phone calls, talking about 'Is everything under control?'" the doctor said. He spoke with tenderness of Victor's wishing to help others and quoted him in a phase he often used, "If I can do anything for you, give me a call". Dr. Watkins ended by saying, "I know the God of Abraham and Isaac and Jacob has said, 'Well done'".

Eulogist Sal Manfre, who worked at Baltimore Contractors for more than four decades, spoke as a representative of the employees. He told how Victor, after the senior Manfre's untimely death (the elder Mr. Manfre had also worked for the firm), had taken him under his wing. "Victor was a second father to me," Mr. Manfre said. "He lived, breathed and eventually died in the business. He was the ultimate sales and marketing person. He expected his people to follow his lead. Most of us tried, but few could really match Mr. Frenkil. He was maybe the last of a breed of dynamic contractors who operated from gut instincts that proved him to be more right than not. Some thought (that style) was intimidating...to get the most from you, to be a leader, a coach... to get people to think

236

and act beyond their normal ability."

The final speaker was the Rabbi Floyd Herman, whose own remarks artfully wove many of the previous speakers' themes into a touching finale. He recalled Victor as "one of the people you never forget, even if you only met him once," possessed of a "wonderful persona". He recalled Victor's delightful "naiveté, his childlike wonder at the world that allowed him to call people at all hours of the day or night without regard to what was happening in their lives".

He then cited Victor's tireless fighting that enabled him to build a successful business, while being kind and generous. The Rabbi praised Victor's people skills — he told his children he had a key to the back door of the White House. He was a man who possessed an innate sixth sense that enabled him to read accurately what was going on about him. This translated into an "incredible business sense". He was bright, energetic and involved, "an entrepreneur all his life".

The Rabbi addressed Victor as a father. He tried to pass on to his children a work ethic — his children were required to work at an early age — and learn a concern for the world around them. "He would drive his children around the poorest sections of town so they could see poverty, to know about the world, the value of a dollar, to know how to make a living," Rabbi Floyd said. "Victor," he said, "was a wonderful father who taught his children about love and living" (even though he left most of the childrearing to Margaret). The Rabbi also noted that being a child of Victor Frenkil was not always easy, "but it was rewarding, and a privilege". He also said he was devoted to his extended family, his brothers and sisters.

He enjoyed the challenges of business, which complemented his personality as a fighter, one who wanted to make the world a better place. "Somehow our sanctuary will be a little bit emptier, our lives will be a little emptier," he said.

Rabbi Herman noted he would miss Victor in his customary place at Har Sinai, seated next to his old friend, Louis Goldstein, who routinely accompanied him to services there during the holidays.

He recalled that the great joy of Victor's life had been his more than 60 years of marriage to Margaret and how her recent passing had exacerbated his own failing health. "His battle with his own mortality was one fight he could not win."

"We'll never forget his smile, his easy way with people, folding bills into monograms. Always it seemed his fingers were busy. His life was a blessing and his memory will also be a blessing," he said in conclusion.

Both Rabbi Floyd Herman and Father William Au officiated at the burial. Word of Victor's death was featured in *The Baltimore Sun*, with laudatory quotations from two Maryland governors. He was hailed as a major builder and philanthropist.

A long, unusual and successful life had finally, inevitably, come to an end. But it ended in a way that would have delighted Victor. The curtain came down on a totally positive note, he was surrounded by those who loved him as he had loved them — and was celebrated on page one of Maryland's most powerful and prestigious newspaper, *The Sun*. In this newspaper, in which he had been scandalized during the investigations of the overages in the Rayburn House Garage, the headline read, "Philanthropist Frenkil, 90, dies".

Victor was front-page news, even at the end.

XIV. The Last Word

"This is not to say that becoming a father automatically makes you a good father....But the urge to be a perfect father is there, because your child is a perfect gift."

Kent Nerburn

Even after all these years, I miss my father. I miss our daily conversations, when he would offer his observations and advice. I miss his standard signoff, "I'll be on tap if you need me". There are many things I miss, and I mention a few of them here.

As I sifted through his personal files, I discovered countless examples of the considerable amount of time and energy he spent helping his four children and numerous grandchildren through the difficult times we all face. I've come to realize that, although not always present physically, he was always there to tackle our problems, without our thanks, as we knew little of his hand in our destiny. I have gained, at this late age, a healthy respect for him as a father, and I miss his wise counsel.

My father was a teacher. Although he didn't always practice what he preached, he was always teaching others what he thought was a better way of doing things. He taught me a lot, such as the dignity of hard work, a strong sense of right and wrong, the need to help those who are less fortunate, that one's word is one's bond, and the value of a dollar.

My father was also a bit of a philosopher. He would write and accumulate short, pithy sayings, many of which he'd have printed on 3x5 cards and placed in his employees' pay envelopes. Typical were: "Do it NOW", "Get the job done", "Be brief but specific", "Keep your eye on the ball", and, perhaps his favorite, "Plan your work and work your plan".

My father was charitable to a fault. He chaired many fundraisers and gave generously to the American Cancer Society, the United Negro College Fund, College of Notre Dame, Associated Jewish Charities, the Boy Scouts, Coppin State College, and many, many more. He also helped his employees by endlessly and discreetly slipping them money, paying for their education and, in some cases, their children's education and, on occasion, their children's weddings and on and on. He was unable to pass even a needy stranger on the street without giving him or her money.

I remember how he would drive my sisters, Janet and Bebe, and my brother Len and me, through the poorest sections of town. He wanted us to see for ourselves how needy some people were — so we could appreciate all of the good fortune we were lucky enough to enjoy. He constantly reminded us that, if you do enough things for enough people over enough years, maybe someday someone will do something for you.

When Dad was in his fifties, he began talking about having a book written on his life, his trials and tribulations, and his ultimate success. Over a period of years, he hired many people to write it. Some were grandchildren who knew him well, others newspaper reporters, secretaries, a college president and even a cab driver. None was a thorough professional. And most gave up in frustration as he changed, rewrote and deleted.

When he died at the age of 90, he still had not seen his

biography completed. Knowing how much it would have meant to him, I decided to complete the book that he wanted so much, but I didn't know where to start. So I called my oldest friend, Tony Weir (who is a professional writer) and asked him for help. His schedule was far too busy to permit him to take on the project in its entirety. And, as he pointed out, we really needed not just

Victor Frenkil, Jr. (with his wife, Nancy), who made this book possible.

a writer but a first-class researcher who could dig through reams of old information, interview many people, track down old newspaper articles and then write a rough draft, which Tony agreed to polish and edit where necessary.

We talked with several writers, but none seemed right until Tony and I met Jacques Kelly, who grasped what I wanted. Jacques is a pro who has worked for *The Baltimore Sun*. And, by chance, he is a history buff among whose favorite subjects are Baltimore and Maryland.

He diligently dug, interviewed, filed, dug some more, drafted and worked closely with Tony (displaying remarkable patience) until, together, they achieved my father's dream. And I have made a good friend in the process.

Let me add that I am forever grateful to my life-long friend, Tony Weir, who patiently held my hand, stirred the pot, added

The tradition lives on: Victor Jr., wife Nancy and President Bush in 2005 after Victor Jr. presented him with "GWB" folded from a single dollar bill.

many of his own thoughts (he knew my father well), then fine-tuned, edited and added to this book. He also did the layout and design of the book and dust cover, and set the type, making it ready for printing. Without his help, I might not have completed what I set out to do. And I owe my sister, Janet, a formal thank-you for her skillful and helpful proofreading.

"Get Me The White House!" is unique to our family and a testament to my father's strength of character. I believe it will help all who read it (but particularly his descendants) learn more about him, how he rose above all expectations and, with any luck, encourage them to raise their sights.

I am proud to have been one of the few he trusted, and I hope that somehow he knows that his trust was well placed now that his wish, after 40 years, has finally been carried out.

Victor Frenkil, Jr.

Glyndon, Maryland

9 October 2005

AFTERWORD

"There is no life that can be recaptured wholly...
which is to say that all biography is ultimately fiction.
What does that tell you about the nature of life,
and does one really want to know?"

Bernard Malamud

Many years ago I realized there were two schools of thought in Baltimore about Victor Frenkil. One said he was a sharp operator and you'd better watch out; the other said he was a self-made genius, a hero for all entrepreneurs.

I didn't know where I stood on this subject until one winter morning I opened the newspaper and read that Victor Frenkil had bought the Belvedere Hotel.

Like so much he did, it seemed to be on impulse. But I was a Victor convert on the spot because he was doing something that appealed to me.

He took the risks that scared lesser people.

As a reporter in my 20s I tried to interview Victor, but he always had so many public-relations people guarding him, I could never quite get a complete sentence out of him. That didn't stop the stories, because there was always something to write about.

I am not alone in believing that, because Victor traveled with such an entourage of people who fretted about what they thought his image should be, the real Victor rarely emerged. Occasionally reporters caught a side or two of Victor; he didn't fit an easy description.

I had one lengthy visit with Victor Frenkil. It was about 1985 in the Belvedere Hotel's John Eager Howard Room. I sat with Victor, his wife, Margaret, and his loyal and devoted secretary and assistant, Virginia Lambrow. Of the three of us, I think it was Victor who did the least talking. I think they tried to talk me into writing a biography of him then.

I ducked the assignment on the spot.

I'd also visited his office at 711 South Central Avenue when he was trying to get a contract for work on a Lexington Market garage. He was worried that he wouldn't get the contract; I thought to myself that it was never in doubt that the contract was his.

On another occasion, I found myself the chairman of a community dinner dance at the Belvedere. Victor heard of this and bought a couple of tables.

I later learned he liked nothing so much as to be getting "exposure," as he liked to put it. I learned that night that he really just could not stay away from people, talking, mixing. At first you might think this was just an ego ploy; no indeed, he honestly liked a good time with friends, some he'd made that night. I'd also say he seemed to like food and music.

The other person who much impressed me was his wife, Margaret. In an odd way, the Frenkils and I were neighbors. They lived for all those years just north of me on St. Paul Street at the Marylander. It was not lost on me that they could have resided anywhere, but, like my own people, had remained in one place. I would often overhear Jerry Gordon, the local grocer, as he got an order ready for Margaret.

I can still see Margaret with her wonderful, easy smile, seated in the basement of the old Hutzler's luncheonette in downtown Baltimore. On those days, she was generally alone, taking a break from her shopping.

Here was a woman who could have taken her Saturday luncheon anywhere, or just as easily gone to the store's very proper tearoom. To my eyes, she seemed the happiest lady in Baltimore as she enjoyed her egg-salad sandwich on cheese toast along with the rest of us.

As I got into the writing, I realized that Victor's son, Bruz (Victor Jr.), could have written this book if he had had a mind to sit still long enough.

I was much impressed by his devotion to his father's memory. So I combed the files and scrapbooks that Virginia Lambrow and her staff had so diligently preserved, and asked Bruz the questions.

Along the way I met his colleagues, who recalled their roles in the Victor Frenkil story. I had some exceptionally good times at restaurants and places like the Club 4100 in Brooklyn, where the spirit of Victor Frenkil was much evident during these sessions.

The Frenkil family, Victor Jr. of course, and Leonard and Janet, as well as nephew John Rouse, were helpful and candid. I thank them as well as Mat DeVito, F.X. McGeady, Charles Benton, George McManus, Virginia Lambrow, Sal Manfre, Father William Au, Pat Dorn, Judge Dulaney Foster, Keith Straley, Edward Hanrahan, Jerry Jarosinski, Dr. Levi Watkins, Jack Jones, Charles Foelber, William Hundley and former governors William Donald Schaefer and Marvin Mandel.

I was also impressed by the time and careful attention that

I was also impressed by the time and careful attention that Stephen Sachs gave in support of Chapter VIII, "Fighting City Hall". His recollections of the events of 35 years ago strengthened the book.

Along the way I met my collaborator, Tony Weir, whose enthusiasm and high standards kept the project moving.

Jacques Kelly
Baltimore, Maryland
15 November 2005

NOTES

Chapter One: Much of this information came from inter-views conducted during the summer of 2003 with James Frenkil, Victor's younger brother. Federal census information from Baltimore's Enoch Pratt Free Library provided the details of the Frenkil household; Baltimore City Directories for the period list where the Frenkil family resided as well as the loca-tions of the Frenkil family business.

Other information about the early years came from several unpublished histories that Victor Frenkil commissioned over the years. His Forest Park High School achievements are well noted in "The Forester," the school yearbook, and are also on file at the Pratt Library.

Nelson Fenimore, one of Victor's closest high-school friends, made a tape recording in the 1980s of his experiences working alongside Victor in the late 1920s. Other details came from Victor Frenkil, Jr., who heard his father tell certain sto-ries on many occasions. He also has the track medals Victor won while a Forest Park student.

Chapter Two: Nearly all the information in this chapter comes from a history that Victor commissioned in the 1980s. He himself told the stories of his episodes at Johns Hopkins.

His brother James also discussed the period in interviews. Among correspondence that Victor saved was a letterhead from his early business correspondence, from Bethlehem Sheet Metal.

Chapter Three: Victor and Margaret dutifully saved keepsakes of their early business career. Margaret's handwritten entries list Baltimore Contractors' first ventures. She also pasted its 1930s advertisements in a small notebook.

Throughout his life, Victor hired photographers to record his achievements. In the Baltimore Contractors files are bound photographic records of the firm's work, including the Trainor Avenue homes and the club basement for Charles F. Brown, the railway executive.

Biographical material on John T. "Pop" Croswell came from articles published on him in *The Baltimore Sun*. Father William Au, a close family friend and pastor of Baltimore's SS. Philip and James Roman Catholic Church, told of Margaret's spirituality in an interview.

Much of the material in this chapter came from Victor's recollections in a 1990s manuscript.

Chapter Four: Margaret Frenkil was a meticulous record keeper. The family retained her date books and household account books, both used as references. Her name also appears on many occasions in Baltimore's newspapers, *The Sun, Evening Sun, News American* and *Jewish Times*.

Audrey Bishop, a *News American* feature writer, who coincidentally resided in the Marylander Apartments where the Frenkils lived, wrote of Victor and Margaret's domestic life in an article published in 1982. The Frenkil children, Victor Jr., Leonard and Janet, all provided important details for this chapter as well. Family friends Clarisse B. Mechanic, Matt DeVito and F. X. McGeady also recalled Margaret's life for this chapter.

Co-author Jacques Kelly met Margaret on several occasions, including having lunch with her at the Belvedere, but recalls often seeing her enjoying a noontime meal at the old Hutzler Brothers department store, where she ate alone, in a basement luncheonette.

Chapter Five: "Life in the Fast Lane" was conceived by co-author Tony Weir and contains the observations of Charles Benton, George McManus, Virginia Lambrow, Sal Manfre, Judge Dulaney Foster, Jerry Jarosinski, Dr. Levi Watkins, Jack Jones, Matt DeVito, Charles Foelber and Edward Hanrahan, in addition to Frenkil family members.

Chapter Six: Victor's ability to fold a dollar was well chronicled in Baltimore newspapers. Two feature photo spreads appeared in *The Sun's* rotogravure magazine, along with news articles. The first article appeared in 1948; the last in 1996. Victor's business correspondence also notes how many requests he fielded for his work. *The Sun* detailed candidate Wendell Willkie's visit to Baltimore in 1940, when Victor may have picked up the idea of folding dollars.

Chapter Seven: The tone of this chapter was set by *Sun* reporter and editor Anthony Barbieri Jr., in a 1977 profile of Victor entitled, "Frenkil, shrewd workaholic, prospers as omnipresent friend of power".

This chapter owes much to interviews with George McManus, Matt DeVito, Judge Dulaney Foster, Deke DeLoach, Kenneth B. Yekstat, and Governors Marvin Mandel and William Donald Schaefer.

Victor's extensive photo collection provided a visual record of his parties at Wilton and the Marylander. Files at Baltimore Contractors contributed guest and invitation lists, as well as personal notes to political candidates. His daily appointment books, kept by longtime secretary Virginia Lambrow, also reveal his schedules and meetings. The story of helping get Walter Jenkins out of Washington came from a memoir Victor himself had prepared in the 1980s.

Chapter Eight: The files of *The Washington Post, Sun, Evening Sun, News American* and *New York Times* provided many details. Interviews conducted in 2003 with Matt Devito, Jack Jones, Paul Walter, George McManus, and William Hundley were crucial. Former federal attorney Stephen Sachs received an early draft of the chapter and provided insightful comments, which were included in the final version.

Chapter Nine: Family members provided their individual recollections as background for this chapter.

Chapter Ten: Sources consulted and interviews held with Victor Frenkil, Jr., Virginia Lambrow, Sal Manfre, Judge Dulaney Foster, Jerry Jarosinski, Dr. Levi Watkins, Jack Jones, Matt DeVito, Charles Foelber, and Edward Hanrahan; also reporter Richard Kucner's *News American* profile of Victor.

Chapter Eleven: Based on interviews with Vita Kencel, James Gentry, Jack Jones, Virginia Lambrow, Edward Hanrahan and Victor Frenkil, Jr., along with newspaper accounts of the period.

Chapter Twelve: Victor's service to local organizations was well documented in newspaper accounts, which were used. Also there was an interview with Coppin State University president Calvin Burnett.

Chapter 13: Based on personal recollections of many family members, plus the obituary that appeared in *The Sun*, June 4, 1999 and the transcripts of the eulogies at the memorial service.

Back cover: Photo of Jacques Kelly courtesy of Kenneth K. Lam.

INDEX

DeVito, Mathias J.: 117-119, 122, 124, 129-131, 158, 159, 245, 248, 249, 250
Dirksen-Hart Building: 178, 182, 184, 185
Dollar bill folding: 67, 72-78, 80-84, 96, 100, 101, 104, 110, 129, 142, 242
Dorn, Pat: 245
Doss, C. W.: 177

Embry, Jake: 167
Enoch Pratt Free Library: 247
Erlandson, Robert: 72

Fagg, Ann: 98
Fallon, George: 167
Fenimore, Nelson: 15, 247
Fernhill Avenue: 4, 8, 9
Finan, Thomas: 112, 113, 129
Fisher, James: 93
Foelber, Charles: 63, 69, 183, 184, 245, 249, 250
Forbes Magazine: 47
Forest Park High School: 11-14, 19-21, 86, 151, 214-216, 234, 247
Foster, Judge Dulaney: 91, 92, 111, 167, 225, 245, 249, 250
Frenkil, Celia: 2, 8, 9, 51, 144
Frenkil, Ida: 2, 51, 144, 155,
Frenkil, Izaak: 2-8, 16-18, 20-22, 36, 37, 88
Frenkil, James: 2, 4, 5, 7, 9-12, 16, 19, 30, 144, 223, 226, 232, 234, 248
Frenkil, Janet (Krieger): viii, x, 34, 37, 44, 45, 48, 53, 144-147, 149, 160, 165, 167, 228, 246, 245, 248
Frenkil, Jennie: 2, 6-9, 21, 63, 104
Frenkil, Leonard: 45, 49, 53, 97, 103, 109, 146-148, 150,

Note on the Typography

This book is set in Adobe Garamond, a classic typeface originally designed by Frenchman Claude Garamond in the mid-16th century. The original Garamond belongs to the family of Renaissance serif typefaces. There have been many variations on Garamond's classic theme over the years — a tribute to its innate grace, beauty and, above all, easy readability. One of the most recent variations is the Adobe version, designed by Robert Slimbach in 1989.